Understanding the Human Mind

Unstoppable Willpower

Jason Browne

Table of Contents

INTRODUCTION 1

WHY THIS BOOK? 3
Why Me? 3

CHAPTER 1: WHAT'S WILLPOWER AND WHERE DOES IT COME FROM? 7

WHAT IS WILLPOWER? 8
WHERE DOES WILLPOWER COME FROM? 9
IS WILLPOWER FINITE? 12
CAN WILLPOWER BE STRENGTHENED? 13
How Strong Is Your Willpower? 19

CHAPTER 2: THE HALT PARADIGM: HOW WE LOSE WILLPOWER? 25

HALT: WHAT'S MAKING US LOSE WILLPOWER? 26
HOW TO USE HALT METHODOLOGY 30

CHAPTER 3: CAN WILLPOWER BE STRENGTHENED? 35

"USE IT OR LOSE IT" 36
KNOW AND PUSH YOUR LIMITS 37
GOAL SETTING 40
CONTROLLING YOUR THOUGHTS 42
ONE CHANGE AT A TIME 45
TAKE CARE OF YOUR BODY 48
DEALING WITH TEMPTATIONS 50

CHAPTER 4: WHEN BEING TOO GOOD CAN HAVE A NEGATIVE EFFECT 53

BEING TOO GOOD 53
FINDING A BALANCED APPROACH 54
A BIT OF INTROSPECTION 56

LESS IS MORE 58

SO, WHAT SHOULD YOU DO? 60

   Are You Being Too Good? 65

**CHAPTER 5: WHAT I WANT VS. WHAT I NEED—DELAYED
GRATIFICATION AND LONG-TERM HAPPINESS 69**

THE IMPORTANCE OF WILLPOWER 70

IMMEDIATE GRATIFICATION 72

DELAYED GRATIFICATION 73

THE BENEFITS OF DELAYED GRATIFICATION 85

WHY IT'S SO HARD TO WAIT 87

STRATEGIES TO INCREASE YOUR ABILITY TO DELAY GRATIFICATION 89

**CHAPTER 6: WILLPOWER IS JUST THE BEGINNING— BUILDING
GOOD HABITS 99**

UNDERSTANDING WILLPOWER 101

HABIT FORMATION 102

TURNING WILLPOWER INTO LONG-TERM HABITS 103

   Think About It 104

   Does It Matter? 106

   Shift Your Focus 107

   Small Steps 108

   Stack Good Habits 110

   Novelty Tasks 111

   Reward Yourself 112

   Account for Yourself 114

   Replace Motivation 115

   The Joy Yardstick 116

CONCLUSION 119

YOU ARE SKILLED 120

   Willpower Is Made to Share 121

REFERENCES 123

Introduction

"With but few exceptions, it is always the underdog who wins through sheer willpower."

~ Johnny Weissmuller

Have you ever been stuck? Whether stuck physically as in the elevator stopping between floors, struggling to get out of your undersized jeans, or parked in on both sides and unable to get out of your car—you've been stuck. It's the worst feeling on earth: wanting to do something but being unable to. Needing to go somewhere and being restrained. We all know this sensation when it comes to a physical blockage, but what about mental blockages?

Getting stuck is something many of us struggle with in our mental lives too. We want to do something, but our minds simply won't let us. While we may have everything in our favor: a nice job, supportive friends and family, and perhaps even a college education, we are still grinding our wheels and locked in place. You may not even be the underdog, yet you aren't getting ahead in life either. What is holding you back? In essence, you are stuck!

However, as if to add insult to injury, we see people with a whole lot less going for them race past us on sheer willpower. The underdogs, those people who manage despite the world seeming to stand against them. How do they do it?

Are we lost, lacking motivation, or undisciplined? Do we simply lack the drive to persevere despite the odds? You may be no stranger to these questions in your life. Many people feel lost and engage in self-chastisement, blaming themselves for being weak willed or not good enough since they can't stick to their plans or achieve the goals in their lives. You are not alone!

Is having a strong willpower something you either have or don't? Like being born with a massive Einsteinian IQ, and perhaps you are clever or not, wise or not, strong or not? Are you simply doomed to be a weak-willed person for the rest of your life, never achieving what you set out to do?

NO!

Willpower is a muscle. No, not a physical muscle, and it's not in any specific spot in your mind either. It's a skill you cultivate, a habit you develop. In this book, you are going to meet, know, and develop your willpower to new and awesome levels as you achieve more, persevere despite any odds or perceptions, and accomplish your dreams. You can!

Why This Book?

Willpower isn't a new concept, and there have been many books written on the subject. So, why this book? Here, you will learn what willpower is, how to practically improve yours, and discover what threatens it. With real-world examples, you will get to know willpower like never before, make a friend and champion of yours, and you will find the inspiration to create new and willpower boosting habits.

I am not going to try and impress you with jargon words like "subconscious drive" or "locus of control." There are plenty of books out there that can explain the topic with high minded words and "I want to impress you" language. Instead, I'm real, and I want to share my real experiences with willpower with you.

Why Me?

So, why read my book? What makes me the right person to tell you all about willpower? My name is Jason Browne. I'm a 40-something, and all my life, I've been told I should amount to great things since I am intelligent and educated. You could say I have a lot going for me, and, therefore, I should have been at the top of my game in life. I wasn't.

I was falling from one idea to the next, from one endeavor to the next. In reality, I had become a rolling stone, and I wasn't gathering any moss or finding my place in life. Whatever I seemed to do, I lacked the willpower to achieve success in it.

So, I stopped.

Finally, I realized my lack of self-discipline and consistency were sabotaging my life, my goals, and my success. I did a deep dive into psychology, reading whatever I could get my hands on to find out which approaches would strengthen my willpower and create self-discipline.

I developed a plan, and by sticking to it, I reached success in my mid-30s. Along the way, I developed a lot of first-hand knowledge and experience about the internal strength required to keep on going and working hard without anticipating immediate results. My methods, which I will share with you, are tested out in real life. In my journey to developing an indestructible willpower, I discovered a few things:

- Having good intentions isn't enough
- Sharing this knowledge and helping others have become my passion
- Anyone has the potential to change their lives for the better with the right knowledge and training
- Willpower is not something you are born with; you earn it, you grow it, and you develop it
- With willpower, the world becomes your oyster

This is what I offer you here: You will develop amazing willpower and the ability to set goals, reach them, and achieve the most incredible life of your dreams. I'm not going to lie and tell you it will be easy. Instead, I promise, developing real willpower will probably be the hardest thing you've ever done, but you can and will do it. With an authentic and strong willpower, you can do anything! Like the saying goes: the underdog wins through sheer willpower.

Chapter 1:

What's Willpower and

Where Does It Come

From?

Have you ever wanted to do something but didn't? You most likely knew exactly what action was required, and you probably knew there was a reward at the end of this action, but you simply didn't lift a finger to move forward. We've all been there. Whether it's losing weight, applying for a better job, enrolling for a life-changing night course, or changing to a healthier diet ... sometimes, we're just not willing to do it. We lack the willpower to do it.

If you were to consider willpower as two words, you would be left with will + power, meaning you must want something **and** you must give (or have) the energy or power to achieve it. Without the power to move forward on the thing you want, you achieve nothing, and you lack that magical quality of having forward momentum in your life. You lack willpower.

What Is Willpower?

While most of us have some understanding of what willpower is, we may end up providing an endless stream of synonyms for it: self-discipline, drive, resolution, commitment, and dedication. Willpower is about resisting temptation to achieve a longer-term goal. This means you don't let yourself do what you may want to do right now, so you can do or have a better reward in the more distant future.

For instance, you stop yourself from falling asleep while studying (which may alleviate your need for rest now) so you can enjoy a much bigger reward later (like completing your degree and getting a better job). There are many other examples of willpower in our daily life, and you have been using it for a very long time, often without even thinking of it:

❑ You decide not to eat the extra slice of cake (a sweet reward now) to be able to fit into your bikini this summer (a long-term goal).

❑ You save money (instead of spending it on things now) so you can have enough to go on a boat cruise in two years' time (a much bigger goal).

❑ Your friend invites you to join them on a Vegas road trip (which would be an awesome experience) as you want to stay home and work an unpaid internship at a well-placed non-profit organization (a career advancing move).

From these examples, you discover two common denominators: choice and restraint. You have the ability to choose to do something or not do it. This choice is informed by your goals, your ability to think forward, and future plan(s). In essence, it is about the value you assign to something: a cupcake versus looking stunning on the beach.

Willpower is a skill that influences all other skills. Want to ride a bike—your willpower will determine whether you get up every time you fall off until you master riding the bike. You want to do something (ride a bike) and you will yourself (choose) to do it. Having willpower also means you refuse to give up (willing not to do something). Why do we have such a complex mechanism to determine what we do? Where does it come from?

Where Does Willpower Come From?

Having the ability to control your own actions based on a decision is what separates us from lesser creatures, and while a dog may be trained to sit and wait, this is again only due to human intervention. We have an internal mechanism that allows us to self-regulate our actions. Hence, we can decide to do something that may be slightly unpleasant if it brings us a greater reward later.

Ok, so we do need a little science here:

Willpower may seem like some abstract concept, but scientists have actually been able to find where it is located in your brain. If anyone has ever tapped you between the eyes and said you needed to think when you were lacking in motivation—they're not far off. This is where your prefrontal cortex (PFC) is located. It is the part of your brain responsible for abstract thought, thinking about thinking (which is pretty unique to humans), and emotional and behavioral regulation. Basically, it is where you plan, consider, and feel—all those things that make you human and motivate you.

The PFC is the part of your brain responsible for advanced thought, and it allows you to decide to delay gratification to obtain a reward you value more. The theory that the PFC is responsible for willpower was first posited after the curious case of a man who suffered a severe brain injury to this section of the brain in 1848. Phineas Gage suffered an injury where a metal rod penetrated his brain, severing the connection to the PFC. While he survived the ghastly injury, he was reported as having had a severe change in personality—changing from a man who was a dedicated worker and well-liked to a man without motivation who developed a problem with alcoholism. This ground-breaking study proved the involvement of the PFC in willpower (Cherry, 2020).

We know from related studies that the PFC controls how we think (reason), how we act (what we do), and what we learn from our actions (higher development). Sadly, this part of the brain only reaches maturity around the age of 25, which is perhaps one of the reasons (combined with a lack of experience) why teenagers will engage in risky behavior. They chase instant gratification with drug addiction and give in to peer pressure as they can't yet fully evaluate their actions and make decisions that lead to a larger delayed gratification. Kids have problems with self-discipline and emotional regulation as they have not yet developed the capacity to engage in abstract thought (their PFC hasn't matured yet).

When you are pushing yourself against the odds to achieve a higher goal, such as studying late while all your friends are partying to get a college degree and get a better job, this is the PFC at work. As the early research into Phineas Gage proved, when the PFC is in any way compromised, it leads to altered or deficient willpower.

This does not mean you might have brain damage since you have poor willpower. You do not need a brain scan. Instead, you need to go to the gym—the brain gym. Willpower is more like a muscle (which can be trained) than an either/or gift (either you have it or you don't). Fortunately, willpower isn't something that can be used up.

Is Willpower Finite?

Have you ever been so weary, so tired, that you simply can't think anymore? Brain drain is a real concern to those who exercise their willpower often. This happens, especially after you have been focused on using your willpower continuously and then slip up with other situations that may require your willpower. Imagine studying non-stop to earn that college degree, but as a result of your willpower being weakened, you start over-eating while you study.

One scientific example testing this was a study by Roy Baumeister, a social psychologist, in 1996 (Villarica, 2012). Participants in the study were offered the temptation of chocolate cookies but not allowed to eat them. The test group were told to eat radishes instead. In the follow-up puzzles, the participants who ate chocolates were far out performing their radish-eating counterparts. It seems then, we can become fatigued in our willpower, and our motivation can indeed be drained (at least temporarily).

Willpower is not used up or completely depleted. However, like a muscle, it can become tired after repeated and taxing use, especially when there is no reward offered. However, with sustained reward-based learning, willpower can increase, building in power like a muscle being trained. This describes a theory known as learned industriousness (The British Psychological Society, 2015). In essence, you become more motivated following exercises that require willpower but are rewarding.

The idea that you should be strong-willed permanently is not feasible. As with all organic processes, it fluctuates. Managing it effectively may be the real secret behind having an amazing willpower. We certainly know now that the concept of ego depletion (where we run out of willpower) is not necessarily accurate. So, is it possible to develop a sustained and strong willpower?

Can Willpower Be Strengthened?

If we continue with the analogy of willpower being like a muscle, then it holds that our willpower-muscle can indeed be trained. This means we can strengthen and develop our willpower. I certainly found this to be true in my own life. While I had been falling around from one idea to the other, while never accomplishing much in my twenties, I began training my willpower and achieved my goals in my mid-thirties.

Willpower is when we have the motivation to choose to do something. Strengthening our willpower has a lot to do with our motivation then. You can work on making your self-discipline and self-control muscle stronger. This is a form of brain-train.

There are various strategies and techniques that can help you save your willpower from being unnecessarily depleted while also improving its capacity through habit forming activities. Not sure what this means? It's easy to do daily fitness training when it is a regular routine; however, deciding to do it in the beginning is much harder and draining of your willpower. So, let's look at some techniques to engage in strength training your willpower:

- **Avoid Willpower Strain/Drain**

Willpower abuse can lead to mental burnout. When you have to constantly exercise your willpower, you will cause mental muscle strain. So, avoiding abuse of your willpower is about limiting the unnecessary decisions you have to make. It is surprisingly easy to start doing this. Essentially, you look at all the unnecessary decisions you make on a daily basis and preplan them, choosing generic solutions to take the "thinking" out of those decisions.

You might pre plan to eat the same food for lunch every day, limiting the need to decide on what you want to eat. Or, you might pre plan the menu for your week, enabling you to only think about this once, instead of struggling with the decisions every day. Decisions you can pre plan or eliminate completely include what to wear, what to avoid, routines such as which route to follow to work, days for certain activities, etc.

- **Focus With Imagination**

Imagination is a powerful force. When you can visualize the rewards for something you are working towards, you are using your imagination to help your willpower remain strong in the face of temptations. Imagining yourself driving a brand-new car after you manage to get your degree and land a good job is one way of keeping yourself motivated and boosting your willpower.

- **Mental Distractions**

When you are trying to boost your willpower to avoid doing something such as when you diet and want to avoid thinking about sweets and greasy foods, then you can use mental distractions to remain resolute. Instead of focusing on what you are denying yourself, you think about completely different topics. While you are trying to avoid thinking about spending money, for instance, you can rather occupy your mind with word puzzles or even see yourself peeling vegetables somewhere.

What we think of gains power over us. If you think about not eating chocolate, you will not deter yourself; instead, you will focus yourself to see chocolates everywhere. Thinking about the things you need to stop doing will most likely lead to us doing those things, like binge eating and other deviant behavior. Rather distract yourself from thinking of those things, stripping them of all power.

- **The Knowledge of Good Habits**

When maintaining and developing a strong willpower, you need to cultivate skills and habits that support positive development. When you are feeling stressed and tired, your willpower will suffer. By finding positive habits and skills to manage stress before you feel yourself heading to a nervous breakdown, you will maintain strong willpower.

Learn to engage in self-care to help diffuse your stress. Identify stressors and find meaningful ways to deal with them. When your body is stressed, it creates stress hormones such as cortisol, and you will have to find ways to diffuse the tensions you feel when you are being flooded by these hormones and neurotransmitters. Listening to calming music, going for a run, taking a yoga class, having a nap, and watching a comedy show are all great ways to diffuse tensions.

Worrying about money is a common stressor, and it might mean you need to develop a stringent financial management plan. If you struggle with and stress over your taxes, then you need to use a small amount of willpower every week to collect and file all your documents and receipts instead of waiting for the end and the chaos that drains your willpower.

- **Incremental Approach**

Feeling overwhelmed by a particularly stressful situation is what leads to stress overload, causing your willpower to fizzle. Imagine being born and as soon as you can walk, you are told to go run a marathon. If you could understand the magnitude of the task, you would probably have a mental meltdown then. Yet, dealing with overwhelming tasks is simply a step-by-step process. You place one foot in front of the other, and then another foot and another.

It is looking at the overall magnitude that knocks the wind from our sails. Many successful people will tell you how they don't look at the whole task. Instead, they take it one bit at a time. By consciously breaking a large task down into smaller tasks, you maintain a steady level of motivation and willpower. This approach allows you to celebrate each step, build up energy for the next, and keep going. The upside of this method is that instead of feeling burnout at the end, you will have a feeling of "what's next."

- **Be Authentic**

If you don't normally wear high heel shoes, then suddenly wearing them will tire you out completely. This is because you are trying to do or be something you are not. The same holds true for your personality. If you aren't a certain type of person, then pretending to be like that will only drain you and lead to demotivation and a breakdown of your willpower reserves.

Knowing yourself is the first step to being authentic. It's like finding the most comfortable pair of shoes, and now you can walk miles in them without much effort. Being authentic is how you turn the tap off that is leaking out motivation on falsehood. Knowing who you are, what you want, and what you are willing to do will help you maintain and grow your willpower.

Being a people pleaser or making yourself into "ice-cream" is not going to help you build your willpower. Instead, it drains your abilities as you try to maintain a facade that isn't real.

- **Avoid Temptation**

My friend is a recovering alcoholic. And like most alcoholics, she learned at the rehab center to remove all temptations from her life. She no longer keeps alcohol in the house, not even for cooking, and she will not go into a bar to socialize. She knows that when she faces temptation, it drains her willpower. With too much temptation, she is likely to slip up and give in. There can't be an excuse of "it's just one drink" or "just have a sip of mine." She knows temptation is bigger than her willpower, so she avoids temptation.

You should do the same. If you are studying and your friends are in the same room, playing cards or chatting away, then you need to make the choice to leave the room (and the social temptation) and go where you will not be draining your temptation. It's kind of like switching off your mobile phone to save the battery. You switch off the temptations in your life so your willpower battery can last longer.

Don't get out of temptation or disaster; instead, avoid it all together by using a small initial amount of willpower to make a sound decision.

How Strong Is Your Willpower?

We've spoken quite a bit about willpower and knowing yourself now, so how well do you know yourself? How strong is your willpower? I like to equate this exercise to knowing how much gas is in your car before taking a long trip. If you know your tank is full, you can drive with a sense of ease, but if your tank is only half-full, then you may begin to worry you might get stuck and run out. This gas is, of course, your willpower.

Answer the following short questions by selecting a short response:

1. How do you feel about change?

a. I love it and actively seek it.

b. I feel threatened by it.

c. I don't like it, but when it's unavoidable I embrace it.

***

2. What type of planner are you?

a. I plan for most eventualities, allowing room for adaption in my plans.

b. I don't plan because life is chaotic anyways.

c. I have a basic plan, and I mostly stick to it.

***

3. **What do your goals normally look like?**

a. I choose a major goal with smaller steps leading up to it.

b. I don't believe in goal setting; life just goes where it wants anyway.

c. My goals are usually huge, and I seldom reach them. But it's still fun to dream.

***

4. **Do you have supportive people in your life? Have you created a management system to help you cope with challenges?**

a. I know I can't do everything alone, so I know who I can turn to for help and also who I should avoid as they bring temptations into my life.

b. I do it alone. I was born alone, and no one is going to help me get ahead except me.

c. Usually, I get stuck and then have to look for people who can help me. I most often end up using professional services to help me cope.

***

5. **With your current discipline system, can you resist immediate temptation, or do you buy stuff you like as soon as you see them?**

a. I notice things I want or need, then I evaluate whether I can afford them now or if I should plan ahead and purchase it later.

b. Yeah, I see it, I buy it. You only live once, you know.

c. I might buy stuff if I have money for it right now. But I'll never go borrow money or go into debt to buy something.

***

6. You are asked to list three positive characteristics you have.

a. You can quickly think of at least three characteristics such as being kind, hardworking, enthusiastic etc.

b. You don't know what to say. After all, you shouldn't just flatter yourself like this.

c. You manage to get two characteristics, but you are a bit stumped when you have to think wider.

***

7. Do you have any resolutions to be healthier?

a. Yes, I know I need to take care of my health, so I am currently on a low-fat or low-carb diet combined with a light exercise regimen.

b. No, I live my life, and I'm not going to cut things out that I like.

c. I intend to be healthy, but I struggle to avoid unhealthy choices.

***

8. When you hear temptation's call, do you give in a little or find something to distract yourself with?

a. When I am tempted to have a drink when I had promised myself not to, then I stick to my promise. Instead, I might reward myself for choosing the right choice.

b. I don't think anything is wrong with giving in just once. It's only one drink, after all.

c. When I am tempted, I give in. I don't want to struggle through life, and if I can enjoy the moment, then I will.

***

9. You are stressed, and when you realize you are heading to the edge of the mental meltdown abyss, you decide to make some changes. What do you do?

a. I consult with professionals to help me make appropriate changes and I include these in my day planner, sticking to these as closely as possible.

b. Knowing I need to relax, I start hanging out with friends and enjoying a weekly drinks session.

c. I read up on self-help, but most of it seems too impractical, so I will try and take a meditation retreat one day when I'm ready.

***

10. **While you have quit a bad habit, you still have friends who persist in that habit. Do you avoid them or ask for their support in helping you not engage in that habit?**

a. I speak openly to my friends about their habit and how I want to make changes in my life. They support me as they see it means a lot to me.

b. I know my friends will laugh at me, so I keep quiet and try to do only a little of the bad habit.

c. Avoiding the habit I used to practice, I try to avoid my friends since I know they will not understand.

Score yourself:

A—letter A answers score 3 points

B—letter B answers score 2 points

C—letter C answers score 1 point

A score of 25-30: You are resilient, and you find ways to keep your motivation strong. As a result, you have developed a strong willpower. By carefully managing your responses to the world around you, you have learned to stick to your guns, plan effectively, and you communicate well.

A score of 15-24: You can show instances of willpower, and while you don't like being pressured, you do often compromise. Quitting bad habits is tough for you, and you usually backslide. You tend to be a people pleaser, and if you are pressurized, you fold like a deck of cards. Most of your goals are never reached.

A score of 10-14: You lack willpower. Mostly, you cruise through life, never accomplishing much. By living now, you may believe you are living in the moment; however, you are simply accepting everything that comes your way. When challenged, you always take the easy way out. You need other people to set goals for you, and you will probably not do well as a self-employed person.

Now that you know what your strong points and weaker points are, let's deep dive into what makes us lose willpower.

Chapter 2:

The HALT Paradigm: How

We Lose Willpower?

So, willpower is not some imagined "have it or don't have it" concept. We know it is located in the prefrontal cortex, and we know it has a biological component. Like the curious case of Phineas Gage showed us, damage to the PFC can lead to life altering changes and a severe impediment to willpower. And while this was a severe case, and not many of us will end up with a metal rod passing through our brain, there are still other reasons why we could lose our willpower.

In essence, it boils down to HALT: Being *hungry* or eating a nutrient deficient diet, feeling *angry* or emotionally unstable, suffering from feelings of *loneliness*, or feeling too *tired* to care and use your willpower. Psychologists have been studying these factors that so easily make or break our willpower and much is known about them. Unchecked, these HALT factors can slowly eke away at your discipline and self-control until you no longer feel empowered enough to use your willpower. These interconnected factors can so easily and insidiously influence our ability to think, plan, and feel that we lose all willpower.

HALT: What's Making Us Lose Willpower?

Willpower is quite literally about moving ahead, and when certain needs are not met, we grind to a halt. If we are hungry, angry, lonely, or tired, we tend to simply spin our wheels in the moment and we lose forward momentum. I certainly became really well acquainted with these factors in my early twenties. While I struggled to find my place in the scheme of things, I soon realized that when I wasn't taking care of my body, and not acknowledging my emotions, I ended up feeling lonely, and soon, fatigue would set in.

By understanding each of the HALT factors, we can better monitor ourselves and be prepared to take steps to counter the willpower drain from happening.

- **Hungry**

While actually being hungry at this moment may not necessarily impact on your willpower, placing yourself on a starvation diet certainly will. When you are denying your body the nutrients it requires such as carbohydrates (in moderation) and fatty acids (in moderation), you are limiting the chemicals your brain can produce. Without the correct chemical mix in your brain, you will struggle to produce feel-good hormones and neurotransmitters that control your mental processes. Basically, you are putting your brain on protest action.

Eating a balanced diet will ensure your brain is able to produce the controlling chemicals, hormones, and neurotransmitters you need to make rational decisions instead of letting your emotions run away with you. An emotional you will not be able to exercise self-control or practice discipline. When the delicate balance between the hippocampus (our emotion factory) and the PFC is disrupted, chaos will ensue. Research has shown that syrup and sugars increase the production of stress hormones (Lino, 2020). This isn't good for you as it drains your willpower even further, making you become emotional and engage in emotional decision making.

Make slow changes, including the things you need and cutting out some of the things you don't. Replacing a cup of coffee a day with a cup of green tea will not light up the fires of mental protest. However, suddenly quitting coffee cold-turkey may drive you off the emotional cliff. While it may seem like a good idea to start a new low-calorie diet when you start your new job, you may find this negatively affecting your self-control and discipline, and your willpower could end up being at an all-time low. While cravings are not a good thing, going boot camp on your body will conversely turn it into a sulking teenager who only wants junk food and chocolates. Your body will also only want to satisfy other unhealthy cravings. Slowly make the changes you need, embracing a healthier you one step at a time.

By adding exercise to the dietary needs of your body, you will also further trigger the production of serotonin and other feel-good chemicals to help you feel positive and motivated to make the right decisions in your life.

- **Angry**

When we are angry, most of us scream, shake our hands, sweat, and bare our teeth. We are, in essence, exhibiting a very primitive picture. Primitive man wasn't able to show the same levels of self-control and discipline as we have today. The caveman didn't have a need for willpower, self-discipline, or restraint. There was no future plan and no journey to success. Fortunately, we have evolved, and being able to control our ego and show strong and positive willpower is what separates us from the caveman.

Negative emotions such as anger, jealousy, hate, or anxiety can cause us to revert to more primitive mechanisms such as the fight-or-flight response. This causes your focus to shift from long-term goals to a short-term gratification of needs. You react to a need instead of responding to a question. You could likely find yourself going on a shopping spree since you feel angry at your ex or quitting your job since you feel jealous of your colleague. By being emotional, you lose the ability to exercise your willpower.

- **Lonely**

Having people you can turn to in times of need and to support you is part of having the elements you require for success. Feeling like you are alone or being lonely is not beneficial for your willpower. Having supportive friends will charge your motivation, keep you grounded, and help you focus on what needs to be done. Friends can also help you celebrate the times when your willpower has remained strong and helped you overcome temptation.

- **Tired**

Being fatigued, whether from lack of sleep or being overworked, is not good for your mental reserves. There is only so much you can take or give before your willpower becomes strained and eventually drained. Knowing when to stop and rest is essential for maintaining healthy motivation levels, keeping your willpower strong, and remaining in charge of your actions.

Make sure to get enough sleep, rest periodically while your willpower recharges, meet your social and support needs with friends who are committed to your life goals, eat healthily, and avoid negative and draining emotions. By aligning these factors, you will give yourself and your willpower the best chance at success.

How to Use HALT Methodology

So, apart from the really cool acronym, what do you do with the HALT methodology? How do you apply it in your life? When you feel your willpower slip, you may already have waited too long to intercede and try and reel yourself in. Instead, the principal of the HALT methodology is to stop regularly throughout your day and engage in self-assessment. This is to help you track your feelings, state of mind, and stress levels. It helps you remain in control and avoid losing control altogether. Often, we may find ourselves feeling angry or upset at something trivial, only to find that we have skipped a meal and our calorie intake has dropped. In essence, like a hungry baby who cries for attention, we may be getting angry or becoming impulsive because a simple need is not being met. It is important to make sure your body runs at optimal levels if you are to give your willpower the best shot at being in control.

The HALT methodology has been used successfully in addiction support groups, and it has helped many alcoholics and drug addicts in their recovery process. In essence, it is about stopping and self-evaluating throughout the day, thereby reducing the chances that you will lose self-control due to either being hungry, angry, lonely, or tired. If you can ensure these basic needs are met, then your chances at maintaining self-control and keeping your willpower strong increase dramatically.

So, how do you do a HALT check?

For each of the letters, you might stop and ask yourself these questions, being aware of how you respond and feel to each. You might make this a meditative practice to do a few times a day. If you can turn this into a habit or pre-flight check before you make a decision, you increase your chances of staying strong in your willpower.

Hungry

1. When last did you eat?
2. What did you eat?
3. Are you feeling light headed or dizzy, indicating a possible low blood sugar level?
4. Are you being tempted to eat something you have decided to give up?

Angry

1. How are you really feeling at the moment?
2. Are you experiencing tension, raised muscle tone, hormonal changes, rapid breathing?
3. Do you feel comfortable thinking about and talking about your feelings right now?

Lonely

1. When last did you spend quality time with a friend?
2. Did you receive messages from a friend today?

3. How often do you speak to your family?
4. What was the last nice thing your friends or family did for you?

Tired

1. How many hours did you sleep last night?
2. When last did you allow yourself to have a nap?
3. Do you wake up feeling refreshed?
4. Do your dreams upset you?

Using the HALT technique is about creating pauses in your life, not just on grand occasions like New Year's or on your birthday, but also on a daily level where you can stop and think, planning ahead for what you want to achieve and how you will do that. This is how you defuse stressful situations, get your logical mind on track, and prepare your brain for what it needs to think and do. By overcoming instinctual urges to emotional eat, snap at what you see as confrontational, and flee from what you perceive as threatening, you can allow your brain to assert control over your body.

When you HALT, you realize that the new system being used at work, while it may seem threatening, is not out to get you and there is no need to flee. You can allow your brain to think logically, plan your steps forward, and anticipate the results or effects of your actions. Acting without thinking is what keeps us stuck in a rut or out in the cold.

By being mindful of your needs, you can stave off temptations (Willard, 2017). You can take ownership of your actions instead of having your willpower fail and reacting. In my life, I often reacted to what was happening around me, instead of acknowledging how I was feeling, which was dictating my actions to me. Only once I began to use the HALT methodology, knowing my own state of mind, the condition of my body, and the needs that were influencing my decision-making paradigm did I start to make logical decisions and use self-control to guide my life in line with my willpower.

Chapter 3:

Can Willpower Be Strengthened?

People fall into two categories: those who train and those who don't. You may decide your body needs work, and therefore, you go to the local gym or you hire a fitness trainer or dietician to help you meet your diet goals. Or, you have given up, not caring what you eat or the results thereof, letting yourself sink into excessive and unhappy behavior. Whichever of the two groups you fall into, you have chosen it. Take a moment to let that sink in … you have chosen it. No one forces you to eat and no one forces you to train.

The same holds true for our willpower. Like a muscle, it can be trained or neglected. However, it is your choice which of these two paths you walk. You may choose to create a healthy and happy willpower that serves you in life instead of letting yourself choose to engage in reactions and failed resolutions. You choose.

Luckily, science and psychology have discovered the nature of our willpower, and we can now make an informed decision. It becomes easier to choose when you know exactly what you are letting yourself in for. It is possible to increase your self-control and build your motivation levels to make healthy decisions on a daily basis. Here's how:

"Use It or Lose It"

Tom was a dear friend of mine. We had similar habits, and while I began training my willpower in my mental gym, he chose not to. For Tom, being in control and showing self-restraint wasn't that important. Perhaps he didn't really feel we could control our decisions anyway. He was hot-headed, quick to get angry, and easy to jump to conclusions.

He would quit at least three jobs a year, and he often found himself at odds with his friends, believing they were against him. Pretty soon, Tom had put on 60 pounds, and he had developed a risky drinking habit. I've lost contact with Tom, but every so often, if I do see him, I am struck by how unhappy he seems to be, hauling his ever-increasing girth with him while he looks at the world with sad eyes. Fight-or-flight mode had become Tom's modus operandi.

Why do you need to know about Tom? You see, there was very little difference between Tom and myself, except for the choices we made. I chose to use the HALT method, realizing where I was going off the rails and pulling myself back on track, while Tom didn't see the need to engage in self-reflection and meditation.

With willpower, like with most of our body, it really is a case of use it or lose it. The more you exercise your willpower in a healthy way, the stronger it gets. The trick to choosing and using your willpower is in being kind to it. Like the skinny kid who goes to gym for the first time, you need to know you aren't going to be up there with the big boys who have been going to the gym for years. You simply don't have those mental muscles yet. Over-facing your willpower and using it more than you are used to will only lead to mental muscle strain and stop your progress in its tracks. In building your willpower, you really should focus on preserving and not using (losing) it, and you should never abuse it either.

Know and Push Your Limits

Ego depletion or willpower burnout is a real threat to anyone who is developing better willpower. It often happens when you have been using that willpower muscle for too long or on tasks that are too big for you. Avoiding it is how you maintain a steady improvement in your willpower capacity and self-discipline. To avoid your willpower or ego depletion, you need to know your limits and push at these incrementally, just like any good athlete would. You don't try to run a marathon when you can't even walk around the block, nor do you try to go to bars when you're a recently sober alcoholic.

Push at your limits, but don't break your willpower altogether.

I want to tell you a story about a man. He was born to an average income family who had great ideals for him. They believed he had been sent to do groundbreaking things, and so he believed it too. However, he didn't set out to change the very foundations of society the instant he could walk. Nope. Instead, he started small, getting together a group of friends who could help him, talking to small groups of people about his revolutionary ideas first. When he knew he could do those, he moved on, doing really miraculous work, becoming even more famous and doing even bigger things. Eventually, he faced temptations that most of us would never have been able to face and remain standing from. Yet, he persevered. His willpower had become so strong, he could do things nobody else seemed capable of. When we read about his life today, we see that he also used times of quiet reflection, resting, praying, meditating, and talking to people he trusted to help him in his life. Eventually, he was able to do great charity work, help people living in poverty, and he even made rulers stop and think. He was Jesus of Nazareth.

Yes, I know you're going to say that He was the son of God, and how can I compare us humans to his works or trials, but if you stop and think about it, we can see the HALT method being used even in the life of Christ. Imagine how much better your life, your decision-making skills, and your self-control will be if you also stop, think, pray (or meditate), and gather a supportive group of friends to help you meet your needs?

Now, I'm not an overly religious person. And whether you are a Christian, Muslim, Hindu, or any other type of religious believer (or even an atheist), we can all learn from a good example. Here are some other examples of knowing and pushing your limits in self-control:

❏ You haven't studied since leaving high school 10 years ago, so you enrol in a weekend short course to see if you still know how to study, hoping to further your career skills.

❏ While you are not very happy with your current job, you stick it out, but at the same time, you start selling shares online, making a few bucks and testing the waters in this line of work.

❏ Despite your salary being quite small, you take out an investment account, putting aside a small amount every month by curbing your spending and doing odd jobs on the side to get extra cash.

The flip side of the know-your-limits coin is to exceed your limits or push the edge continuously. This leads to mental fatigue and ego depletion. Your self-discipline has its limits. Challenging yourself continuously with temptations and tasks beyond your power to achieve is not going to help you increase your willpower. Instead, it will sap your willpower.

By alternating between your comfort zone and your limits, you will be able to train your mental muscle effectively. Anyone who has ever worked with a professional athlete or worked with a sports coach or even worked with a fitness instructor will know that there are days when you do the very best you can, and then there are also days when you do slow maintenance with minimal impact work.

Like stretching an elastic band, you build elasticity and tenacity in your willpower by moving from easy tasks to more complicated challenges to your willpower. If you were to only face off against huge challenges, then you would surely lose heart fairly quickly. In the end, you would become tired and the fortress of your discipline would crumble at your feet. So, how do you challenge your willpower in a safe way that builds it instead of breaking it down? You set goals.

Goal Setting

People like dramatic examples. We write books about people who have accomplished amazing and huge things. Nobody writes about someone who managed to put one foot in front of the other, got through their day, and slowly built themselves up. So, when you hear the term goal setting, I can just imagine all the huge goals, the magical dreams, and the change-the-world ideas that float around in your PFC. But goal setting is not about the final product or the end result that you are visualizing at the moment.

Goal setting is a small and gradual progression of steps that will eventually lead to the ultimate goal you are seeking. For some of us, getting up as soon as our alarm clock wails in the morning is already a huge accomplishment. To build your willpower, you should set small goals that can direct you in the right direction. Each of these goals is a victory. Whether that goal is to finish your college degree, simply to make enough to buy your own car at the end of the year, or to wake up and be at work on time every day of the week, you should celebrate each step.

Crucial to building your willpower to become infallible is to keep one eye on the prize and the other on the route there. You can't be like a donkey that will simply follow a carrot on a stick. Instead, rather think of a series of small goals leading you up to your ultimate goal—like slices of carrots to keep you interested and motivated.

Breaking this down, you could divide a big goal such as getting a promotion into a series of steps or mini goals to help get you there. You might begin by reading the company policy (goal one), taking some online courses to help you become more qualified (goal two), increasing your workload and effectiveness to build a stunning résumé for the company (goal three), and finally, applying for the next promotion post at the company (goal four). There could, of course, be many smaller goals in between these, depending on the level of self-discipline and commitment you have already achieved.

For some people, goal setting might be a step-by-step process, aimed at rebuilding their collapsed sense of self-discipline and control. Jumping to the end goal is a huge mistake, and it's one that will only dump you further off track than before.

Don't try to do too much; instead, focus on the quality of work, not the quantity. Instead of failing at your ultimate goal, you can still pick yourself up when/if you fail at a smaller goal. Failing completely will demoralize and demotivate you.

Believe in yourself, working hard towards each goal as if it is the final goal. When celebrating, you should tell friends, and you should make something special out of it. You have gone further than you did yesterday, and tomorrow, you will take a few steps further still. As your willpower increases, so too can your goals. While you are focused on your goals, you may find temptations cropping up. It may prove really difficult to control your thoughts, and soon, you might lose the self-control necessary to achieve your goals. In these situations, it becomes really important to control your thoughts.

Controlling Your Thoughts

Most of us have, at some stage, been tempted. It's a recurring string of thoughts about the thing you are trying to avoid doing or having. Like the devil's whisper, it strokes your ear, corrupting your mind. All that stands in the way is your willpower. Being able to control your thoughts is one very powerful way to limit temptation's hold on you. By being in control of what you are thinking, you will be able to maintain self-control and set the goals you want to focus on.

Redirecting your thoughts or focusing on something else entirely every time your focus seems to gravitate towards temptation is one way to keep yourself to the path you have chosen. Most of us know physical temptation, and if there is a person you find particularly desirable, you know to avoid close proximity to them lest you be tempted to stray.

Essentially, you have two brains. Dr. Kelly McGonigal, renowned psychologist and author of *The Willpower Instinct*, has formulated some interesting theories about your brain's instincts, thoughts, and how to control these. McGonigal explains that we have both a pleasure and a thinker side to our brains (Van Edwards, n.d.). This means while our brains may compulsively try to think about that which we want or desire (the go-brain), we also have the ability to think rationally and engage in wise actions (the no-brain). While these two halves of our brain tend to argue about what to do, the wiser and rational side wins only as long as it doesn't become tired and worn out. This is basically your willpower.

The question arises then, can you control your thoughts? Can you actively choose to go for a long-term reward instead of instant gratification? Do we achieve more in life if we are able to make ourselves wait for a better goal? Psychologists certainly thought they had found a way to test this hypothesis with the famous marshmallow test.

In the 1960s, Stanford psychologist Walter Mischel performed a social experiment where 90 preschool children were asked to look at a marshmallow for 15 minutes. If they could hold off on eating the treat for 15 minutes, they would be rewarded with a second one. The children who clearly diverted their attention elsewhere managed to wait patiently for 15 minutes and claim the second reward. Distraction was a means of controlling their thoughts.

The second part of the experiment was conducted in the 1990s where the same children, now adults, were evaluated in terms of their life accomplishments. The test results seemed to indicate those children who could wait 15 minutes before eating their marshmallow were more successful in their adult lives. The theory was that self-control showed willpower potential (Calarco, 2018).

However, recent repetitions of this and other social experiments have debunked the beliefs they created somewhat. It has been revealed in follow-up tests that other factors may prove a stronger indicator of willpower and later life success. Social background, parental influence, home environment, and level of schooling may have a much higher influence on your adult willpower development than simply being born with it or in being able to resist simple temptations. Self-control, which is a pretty good indicator of willpower, is not yet matured at a young age, so having strong will as a child may not be an indicator of your willpower as an adult.

One Change at a Time

Having strong and positive daily habits will help you avoid temptations and overtaxing your willpower. A built-in set of regular parameters governing your decisions will remove the need for excessive decision making. However, many of us probably only dream of having an established set of positive daily habits. We read about people who meditate, go for walks, and journal, and we only wish we had enough time to finish a cup of coffee before we are reeling from one disaster to the next in our lives. If this is you, then change is needed.

Reading this, you probably start writing down everything you want to change, and it may even go quite well for a couple of days, until you have a really bad day and you end up right back at square one. What went wrong? After all, you were only trying to change your behavior to become more positive and affirmative.

Change should happen one step at a time. Even deciding to get up 30 minutes earlier every morning so you can quietly sit in meditation before you start your day is already a huge change. Your body, your brain, and your habits will take a while to integrate this into your lifestyle and make it a part of your willpower.

Changing more than one item at a time will only further deplete your willpower.

Once you have changed one thing, and it no longer feels so hard to do it, and you don't have to drag yourself to commit to it daily, you can start changing a second element in your life. This guiding principle is why so many people have failed at going on new diets or going to the gym or basically changing any single element in their lives in the long term. It's not that they didn't try. Instead, they tried too much. They tried to change 101 things, and as a result, their willpower was depleted by all the new decisions they had to make. So rather, change one thing at a time.

So, how do you start? Sitting quietly, allow your mind to reflect on your day from the moment you open your eyes to later that night when you close them again. Identify without judgment which habits are good and which are bad. Here are some habits that may be negative on your list:

❏ You eat breakfast on the run.

❏ Your mom calls, and you tell her you'll call back but don't.

❏ Traffic makes you angry, and you are running late for work.

❏ At work, you escape into Facebook and Twitter instead of doing all you are supposed to for the day. As a result, you have to take work home to finish.

❏ You tell your kids to watch TV while you try to work and cook at the same time.

❏ You meet up with friends after supper for drinks, getting a bit more inebriated than you should.

❏ Getting home, you fight with the kids for not having done their homework.

The list could really be endless. The side of your brain that says "go" will probably have a series of reasons for each of the above habits and why you should keep doing them. It will be up to you to take these bad habits one at a time, and you will have to change them using the "no" side of your brain. Letting your "no" brain focus on one thing at a time will help you stay in control. Trying to say "no" to everything at once will only lead to ego depletion or willpower burnout. So, consider the items on your list, one at a time, and start working on changing the items you consider to threaten your willpower. Once that habit has been changed successfully, you can move to the next. One. Step. At. A. Time.

Take Care of Your Body

Remember to refer to the HALT methodology covered in Chapter 2. When you are tired—rest. If you are hungry—nourish your body. When you are lonely—spend time with positive friends. If you are feeling upset—express yourself in healthy ways.

Your body may be a machine, but it is an organic machine. It needs rest, nourishment, an outlet for stress such as meditation or reading, exercise, and to be cherished. When someone is verging on the edge of their ability to cope with what life has thrown at them and/or when their willpower is at an all-time low, we can often see this in their physical appearance. Their skin becomes sallow toned, and there are the tell-tale lines around the eyes. Overeating and engaging in excesses soon become habitual, and you know they are in trouble.

Taking care of your body is about more than just physical appearances. It is about creating a healthy place where your mind can be settled. A body that is well balanced, follows a healthy diet, and engages in modest exercise is likely to be a good place for your willpower to live. When your body is weak, overweight, and prone to health issues (such as diabetes and high or low blood pressure), your willpower will already be pushed to the limits. Taking care of your body can boost your self-control ability and create stronger willpower.

How do you take care of your body to foster a healthy and resilient willpower? It has very little to do with being perfect. Instead, you should focus on nourishing and soothing tasks to make your body a happy place to live:

→ Eat balanced and nutritious meals. Avoid starvation diets. If you do engage in intermittent fasting, then be sure to do so modestly and make this a celebratory part of your diet, not a resentment filled chore. Take necessary dietary supplements that you may not be getting enough of such as Omega oils and important chemicals.

→ Engage in modest exercise aimed at maintaining your body systems, not necessarily to build muscles or a perfect bikini body. Rather, make sure to stretch your muscles, work and improve your joints, and increase your heart and lung health. Regular exercise increases your dopamine levels, and you will benefit from that feel-good feeling throughout the day.

→ Get enough sleep. Being sleep deprived is one of the surest ways to have your willpower fold like a deck of cards. Make sure you are also getting quality sleep. If you are struggling to fall asleep or have bad dreams regularly, then you should take measures to ease your nerves and improve your breathing rate.

→ Deal with stress before it deals with you. We tend to steam ahead, ignoring the warning signs of stress wearing us down. Find ways to deal with your stressors in a healthy and positive way. Go walking, take up hobbies, and find talk groups who can support you. Whatever you do to let go of stress, be sure to find a way that leaves you healthy, refreshed, and at peace. It is important to take care of your mental health. Suffering from mental fatigue, burnout, or stress is not healthy and can be as damaging to your life as developing a heart condition.

Dealing With Temptations

When you have been careful to know and push your limits in self-control, but you still feel overwhelmed by temptation, you may need to take some drastic steps. Even though you may have set yourself goals, managed to control your thoughts, created healthy habits to help you stay on track, and developed a habit of self-care, you may still feel an overwhelming temptation with something in your life. This temptation can take any form really; the donut shop on the way to work, sleeping longer when you should be studying, hanging out with friends when you should be working on extra tasks, or quitting your job when you feel the slightest pressure at work.

Dealing with recurring temptations require drastic intervention. If you can't manage them, then you should remove them. This may mean driving a different route to work so you don't pass the donut shop, setting an alarm in the room next door (forcing you to get up to switch it off), telling your friends to help you by not inviting you to hang out, and speaking to a professional when you feel like quitting your job.

There's an old saying, "out of sight, out of mind," and this holds true for temptations. If you really struggle to use your willpower and say no to temptations, then you need to remove temptations completely. It's easier to say no when you have taken the object of your desires out of sight. Not seeing it every day will help you focus and give your willpower a break instead of taxing it continuously and causing ego depletion.

Chapter 4:

When Being Too Good Can

Have a Negative Effect

Everything in life is about balance. While you may have been someone who chased instant thrills, you certainly don't want to turn into a terminator, who is so focused on achieving a goal or mission that anything getting in your way gets eliminated.

Too much of a good thing can be equally harmful. While you want to improve your self-control and develop your "no" brain, you need to do so in a balanced way. Becoming a dictator on your willpower will not do you any favors. Nobody needs a health-Hitler or a mind-Mussolini. Life should still be fun and worth living.

Being Too Good

By being too goal focused and denying yourself too many small gratifications, you tend to become somehow less than human. Like a machine, you start clinging to perfection, stunt your emotions, and disconnect from the people around you. You start to micro-manage yourself, and while self-control is a good thing, being overcontrolling is not. You start risking nothing, feeling nothing, become so focused on details you miss the bigger picture, and, in the end, you become miserable. The chances increase that you might slip off the wagon so badly, you end up being completely without any self-control.

Being too overcontrolling may lead to severe damage to your interpersonal relationships and connectedness. You may find yourself feeling really isolated, misunderstood, and unable to relax. Maintaining a balance between control and temptation is about knowing when to allow yourself to give in to temptation and when to stay resolute. In finding a balanced approach to self-control, maintaining your willpower, and giving in to healthy temptations, you can achieve much more in the long run.

Finding a Balanced Approach

It's okay to be tempted by harmless gratifications once in a while. Note the use of harmless. If you are a recovering alcoholic, there is unfortunately no middle ground—it's dry or in the drink. With temptations that ruin or threaten your life, it is better not to indulge them. It wouldn't be okay for a recovering addict to just smoke some occasional pot.

However, if your temptation is more harmless, like going out with friends when you have a load of work to still do, then you can stray a little every once in a while. If you tend to overspend and make impulsive buys, then you can choose to buy a treat or make a frivolous buy (singular) after a period of being good. Should you be on a strict diet, you can celebrate a diet achievement with a slice of cake. In fact, most diets have a cheat day, allowing you to still be human and enjoy mild temptations at least once a week. On an emotional level, we need this. The key here is to not make this a habit. The occasional cheat shouldn't become a daily activity, and it should be a choice, not a slip.

In essence, you should make friends with temptation. By seeing temptation as your enemy, you are making it into the elephant in the room. You turn it into something that is always present, but it is never spoken of. You could even give your temptation a name. Like the classic Simon and Garfunkel song, darkness can be your old friend. Acknowledge it, own it, and manage it. As a result, you will show much more empathy to those who are also struggling with their own temptations (which is basically everybody), and you will be more adept at knowing and managing your own temptations. Being ashamed of your temptations and struggle will not help you at all. It is okay to give in to smaller temptations every once in a while—you aren't a rock.

A Bit of Introspection

When managing your temptations and confrontations to your self-control and willpower, you need to start with a bit of introspection. Look inside, find your truth, examine it, and own it. You need to find the ways in which your thinking has become dysfunctional and learn how to retrain destructive impulses. A lot of what you think about yourself influences how you make decisions, what your feelings are about those decisions, and how you bounce back when you suffer a "failure." It is important to make decisions for the right reasons. While going on a diet to lose weight and improve your health is admirable, going on a diet to keep up with your skinny friends is not.

Introspection is about finding where your values and decision-making paradigm lie. This will help you make rational decisions that are not driven by fear; decisions that will not hold you back from missing out or stop you from enjoying life. While you look inward, find the image or vision of what it is you want to achieve. Fix that in your mind's eye, enabling your willpower to self-reference, remain strong, and have some measure to help you choose when to relax and indulge a bit.

The important part here is to choose to indulge, not to fail and give in, but to choose to enjoy the relief or pleasure of a temptation for a brief while. Introspection will help you know when you need to relax a bit and when you need to let yourself enjoy a treat or a loosening of your self-imposed restrictions for a moment. Momentary gratification should be a reward, not a punishable "offence."

Most of us are also quite competitive, and we tend to go above and beyond what we originally envisioned. A friend I know started walking three miles every day, and while they had originally intended this to be a health choice, it soon became a competition. Walking became running, and the three miles were pushed into six miles in less than a week. Where the daily walk had been a healthy self-care activity, it had now become a competition and even an obsession. The joy at the task had faded, and now, my friend's original conviction has become their slave master.

Obsessions aren't healthy. Above all, they aren't sustainable. Most people who have suffered a nervous breakdown or given themselves over to excesses will admit they had been obsessed before. Creating an unattainable or unsustainable ideal will not help you strengthen your willpower. Instead, it will tire out your willpower and drain all enjoyment from your life. Make sure to keep track of your original goals. Are they still what they were when you set out? While it's natural for goals to change and adapt, they shouldn't become chains that shackle you to a now meaningless objective. You are allowed to change your mind, to adapt, and to redirect your course.

Less Is More

When it comes to willpower, using more of it isn't a good thing. It really is a case of using your limited willpower strategically. Less is more. Becoming fanatical about being strong willed will lead to severe lapses in willpower. Remember, willpower is finite. It runs out. You get exhausted and struggle to say no to the important stuff. Instead of relying on your willpower at all hours of the day, you should instead try to only use small bursts of willpower. Using buckets full of discipline can become harmful, smothering your enthusiasm for life.

When you become too focused on an end goal, you may not be able to see the opportunities that present along the way. So, while having self-discipline is often a good thing, having too much can be like going through life with your head strapped down like a mule. Mastering temptation means you overcome the urge to simply give in without being able to think and evaluate things first. Temptation in itself is not necessarily a bad thing. If you can face it and not feel compelled to crumble, then you can learn from it, grow through it, and achieve more because of it. Fearing temptation may cause you to cling to your discipline and iron willpower, missing out on most of life along the way.

After all, in life, we need to be flexible and adapt to the challenges that emerge. Creating a strong willpower is about giving yourself the skills and gifts to show self-control when you need it and adapt when necessary. Just think of all the overachievers who relentlessly drive themselves in pursuit of their goals, often past the point of sanity. Their health suffers, and their willpower may in the end dissolve completely, rendering them vulnerable to simple temptations such as excessive behavior.

Our thinking may also influence our ability to resist real temptations. If you perceive yourself as a really strong-willed person, you may see yourself as not needing to be prepared or alert to temptation's lure. You may trip up and slide down into unhealthy behavior or relationships without you even noticing it. For example, if you are convinced you have high self-control, you may not even notice that you have become addicted to work, that you no longer have the ability to relax, or that you are living a mentally and spiritually draining life.

Conversely, if you believe you have a weak self-control, and you think your willpower is really low, you may give in to temptations without even trying to resist them. You start to use being weak-willed as an excuse for poor performance or inability to resist society's siren call.

In the end, it may be better not to think about your willpower that much. While you may find this an odd statement, given that you are reading a book on willpower, it doesn't mean you should ignore your willpower. Instead, you should know your limits and push them. However, you shouldn't spend hours lamenting your yielding nature and convince yourself you are unable to resist things that are not good for you. Focusing on aspects you do well is how you avoid becoming a victim. Neither should you pride yourself on being blessed with a herculean willpower. As the saying goes, pride comes to a fall. Instead, balance awareness of your limitations with a process of managing the challenges to your willpower.

So, What Should You Do?

This may be the toughest question for you to ask. What should you do? Having iron willpower isn't good, and when you have a dental floss resolve, that isn't good either. So, what is there to do then? For starters, look inward.

- **Become Aware of Your Emotions**

Feel the feelings you are not so comfortable admitting and find ways to regulate your emotions. Trying to control emotions is like trying to hold sand by squeezing your fist. It'll slip through your fingers the harder you try.

Ask yourself some revealing questions:

1. If you weren't so focused on this goal, what would you do?

2.   How do you relate to
your friends?

3.   Did you ever miss out on
something important because your focus was
elsewhere?

4.   Are you afraid of risking
on something new?

5.   Do you feel comfortable
around new people?

6.   Do you relax easily over
weekends?

These short questions may offer some revealing
answers to you. If you tend to be obsessive about your
self-discipline and your willpower, you will probably
struggle to answer most of these questions. The reality
is that you are focused on a very narrow part of your
life. However, your emotions don't shut down. Sudden
bouts of anger, depression, sadness, and even agitation
may be a sure indication that your emotions are
rebelling against being ruled (and ignored) by an iron
fist.

The final outcome of this may be a sudden and
unanticipated slip into the welcome arms of temptation.
True self-control is not in denying yourself every
possible pleasure and leading a monk-like existence
while you try to achieve your ultimate goal. Instead,
having realistic self-control is about seeing the things
that interest you, knowing which of them will be
harmful to your goal in the long run, and which are

harmless indulgences. These can help you alleviate stress, manage exhaustion, and reward yourself for diligent work. Having too much self-control could lead to long-term regret.

-                           **Dysfunctional Thinking**

Once you have begun looking inward, acknowledging your feelings, and applied some willpower boosting methods, you will begin to notice the landscape of your thinking. It may shock you to realize how dysfunctional your mind can be. Sometimes, you may be tempted to choose an option that might not really be good for you, such as an extra slice of cake versus a glass of water, and choosing an option that makes more sense may be less appealing to you.

This phenomenon is known as cognitive dissonance and while it may seem like a bad thing, it can offer you an opportunity to strengthen or strain your willpower. If we follow our previous analogy that our willpower is like a muscle, then exercising that muscle is achieved through actively deciding when we are faced with temptations. Avoiding temptations removes our ability to decide, and our willpower weakens.

So, while we all want to have incredible willpower, we don't really want to train our willpower as we avoid using it by avoiding temptations. Temptations are opportunities to turn irrational desires into rational habits. Our whole thinking surrounding temptations and challenges to our self-control has then been dysfunctional.

Instead of hiding, we should be facing up to daily challenges that may offer growth opportunities to our willpower. True, this doesn't mean you walk into a bar when you are a recovering alcoholic. Clearly, that's looking for trouble. Instead, you may use milder temptations such as being with friends who have a few drinks at a restaurant to test your mettle.

In reality, it isn't the temptation we should resist but rather our impulse to give in to it. Dysfunctional thinking that insists temptations are evil and should be avoided at all costs has made us into a society of iron will that doesn't really create a happy life.

• **Embrace Creativity**

One of the best ways in which you can beat inflexible willpower is to embrace your creativity. When you look at a situation with a fresh set of eyes, open your mind to let your creative juices percolate, and you allow yourself the possibility that there is a different way to do something—magic happens. Considering alternatives to a problem is how we find solutions. If you are really struggling to stay on track with your goal or to maintain your willpower, you could consider letting your creativity have a go. Not feeling like you are making progress with a new work goal? How about singing a song to celebrate each little step? Perhaps you could even bring your resolution to bear in a creative way. Leaving yourself motivational sticky notes on any treats your partner keeps in the fridge will help you avoid binging without banning all sugar from your house (and declaring WWIII on them).

- **Self-Control in Context**

Having self-control is not the only reason for success. While you may value being in control over your actions, feelings, and habits, you need not focus on only developing your self-control. There are a whole range of other factors that contribute to success, not only self-control. Consider what may make you a successful person, only don't list self-control or willpower. Your answers may include:

→ Being a good communicator

→ Being friendly and empathetic

→ Understanding challenges and finding solutions

→ Using insight and understanding

→ Creating answers with creativity

These are just a few characteristics that influence your value-based thinking when it comes to self-control or willpower. Being rigid and domineering regarding your goals and willpower will deny your characteristics and leave your willpower weakened. Your resolve didn't get to grow and evolve. When working on your willpower, you should keep your health and vitality in mind too. An iron willpower can't help you overcome disease or stress-induced illness, that is up to your motivation and innate characteristics.

Are You Being Too Good?

The problem with being too good at resisting temptations and building an iron willpower is that you probably find a justification for it. While you may secretly or even subconsciously know you have gone too far, you will not admit it to yourself. It's a good idea to do a self-check and assess whether you have become too focused on being in control. Any good thing can become bad when taken to extremes. Ask yourself these questions for a reality check:

1. When someone is having a bad day or they become emotional after something traumatic happens to you, do you relate to them?

2. How long has it been since you had a new experience?

3. What is your creative form of expression?

4. Do you allow temptation in your life?

5.   During your day, do you
        focus only on your goal(s) or on the things you
        think may be keeping you from it?

When your willpower and your attempts to create an
iron self-discipline overwhelms your life, you will be
emotionally closed off to others. Since you are ashamed
at instances when willpower fails, you will likely see this
as weakness in yourself and in others. As a result, you
will lack the ability to connect empathically with others.
You can expect a very lonely and isolated life if
willpower perfection is your goal.

Being open and accepting of failures while steering
yourself in the right direction towards your goals allows
you to experience new and often exciting events. Being
focused only on maintaining your own willpower will
limit the occurrence of chance in your life. Chance or
the unintended can have wonderful results in our lives,
and while we need to have a developed willpower to
achieve, it shouldn't blind us to opportunity. Just
consider some things invented by chance: Teflon, corn
flakes, the slinky, and even Penicillin. Willpower
shouldn't close your mind; it should fuel you to make
the most of opportunity.

Being able to put yourself into something that allows
you to express your feelings is important for so many
reasons. It helps you regulate your stress levels, builds
self-esteem, and helps you communicate. Dancing
(even if you can't), painting (even if you're no Van
Gogh), or drawing (even if Picasso would be ashamed)

is important to help you get in touch with an often-neglected aspect of your mind—your creativity. These creative activities may seem frivolous and a waste of time, but they are essential to developing and meeting all of your needs. Your willpower should allow for these creative expressions, not drive you from them.

Some people play it safe all day long, avoiding temptations as far as possible, and they believe themselves to have a strong willpower when, really, they are afraid. Your willpower should be firm enough to consider temptations and decide not to yield. Avoiding anything outside your comfort zone is not practical or even mentally stable. We need to grow and change, and by changing our environments and at least considering new things, we can change for the better. This doesn't mean you need to engage in random sex, drink like a whale, or eat yourself into four more sizes to gain experience. Instead, you consider and decide. The act of choosing reveals a lot about you. Denying yourself the right to choose by playing it safe will only weaken your willpower in the long run.

Engaging in either-or logic is not healthy. The world isn't black or white; instead, it is an assortment of colors and events. While you may want to focus on the temptations you should avoid only, you probably also need to see your ultimate goal, and if you can sniff some daisies on the way there, you'll be all the better for it. Living with your focus exclusively fixated on one aspect of life will create a very one-sided existence. Tunnel vision is not healthy.

While you may find an abundance of literature, both in print media and online, about willpower, increasing yours, using it, and preserving it, there is still a rather limited view on why having a too strong willpower may be harmful to you. Being too good can be a bad thing. Instead, you should try to lead a balanced life, approaching challenges and goals with the same motivation and energy. Knowing yourself through a process of introspection can help you really understand where you are one sided and where you need to work a little on yourself. In the long run, you may find it is less about how strong your willpower is or how much of it you have and more about how you use it, where you save it, and if you do so wisely.

Chapter 5:

What I Want vs. What I Need—Delayed Gratification and Long-Term Happiness

We have started living in a society driven by instant culture. Everything needs to be instant. Fast food, drive through parties, one-night stands, and many more occurrences of people wanting to enjoy something right now, with very little consideration of the impact of that enjoyment on them. We are almost conditioned into wanting a quick way out with everything in life. As a result, we tend to cling to temporary highs instead of working and persevering to achieve long-term gratification.

The question becomes "What do I *want*?" vs. "What do I *need*?" *Want* is a temporary status, and it changes.

What you want today, you may not want tomorrow. *Need* is a much more permanent condition, where you seek to achieve something more than just a here and now event or item. It's a future investment, and while it requires long-term attention and diligence, it offers rewards and happiness you can only imagine. To achieve that fabled state of bliss requires the appropriate use of a well-developed willpower.

It may seem odd to say you require appropriate willpower, but as we discovered in the previous chapter, having inflexible willpower is not the answer either. You need a willpower that is strong enough to stand against temptations but flexible enough to maintain creativity, adaptability, and vision. Your willpower is what will keep you from slipping into habitually fulfilling immediate gratification or momentary wants.

The Importance of Willpower

Facing temptations on a daily basis is not necessarily a bad thing. It is your reaction to these temptations that determines whether you are meeting your goals or falling off the wagon. Why would you choose something you obviously know isn't good for you? Why would you eat a super-sized burger with the greasiest fries you can find for lunch when you had a huge breakfast already? Is there a reason to go home with someone you only just met at a club, when you hardly know them? Is it really a good idea to max out your credit card at the mall during your lunch break? Why would you have two doubles of scotch at lunch when you know there's a meeting later today? It's really easy: it's fun.

These are all instances of instant gratification. They make us feel good for about as long as they last. While you are sipping the smooth oak-barrel flavor of the scotch, you are content, and the world seems a mile away. Buying bags and bags of joy at the mall makes you forget about the troubles at home, and you feel like something is filled inside yourself. Likewise, going home for some horizontal recreation with a good looking stranger is fun while you're busy, even though you may wake up the next morning, suddenly realizing the stranger is no longer so good looking, and you want to chew your arm off rather than wake them to get off you. And while you are licking the yummy grease from your fingers or wrapping your hands around the soft bun with a juicy patty and double cheese and bacon that snuggles in your hand, you are happy.

Willpower is the only thing that will help you get out of and avoid these sticky situations. With your brain tempted, and once your pleasure centers engage, logic flies out the backdoor. Willpower is the doorstop. It keeps that door closed, letting logic return to your mind, settle in and redirect your path to something more meaningful.

Having a flexible and resilient willpower will help you understand temptations, think about them, and decide why and how to resist the instant gratification they offer. While a burger is delicious, you already had a big breakfast, and your willpower pauses you long enough so your logic can assert itself, making you reconsider and choose something healthier for lunch. Your hormones may be telling you "yes, yes!" when you look at the stranger's perfect body, teasing you to give in and have fun, but logic tells you that you have just started a new relationship, and cheating isn't cool. Shopping and having drinks over lunch: your willpower pauses you long enough so your pleasure centers can disengage and logic can re-engage. You realize these are temporary highs, and you don't need another round or more stuff. Willpower makes you think, reason, and decide wisely.

Immediate Gratification

Right now, you may be feeling hungry. You can imagine eating a delicious pizza with extra cheese and all your favorite toppings, but you are also on a diet, and devouring this massive meal would throw your diet way out. Giving in and buying that pizza, eating it all by yourself, will be a very sad case of instant gratification. While your jaws are munching and your taste buds salivating, you will be in heaven. However, as soon as you swallow the last bite and feel your bloated stomach, you will feel remorse. It will not take long to realize you have failed in reaching a bigger goal you had. You may even be so disappointed in yourself, you end up giving up on your diet altogether.

This is the threat of instant gratification: it isn't about having fun or enjoying yourself in that moment. Instead, it is about how you feel afterwards. Usually, you will find the temptation was something very opposite to your higher goals. While it was fun, it has set you back miles in your journey to achieve upwards mobility.

That double scotch may cause you to perform badly in the post-lunch meeting. You will not impress your future boss, and this will cost you the promotion you had been working so hard for. Buying all that stuff at the mall may cause you to go into further debt, setting you back from being able to afford that holiday you had planned with your family.

There are many ways in which giving in to instant gratification can be bad for you in the long run. While it may seem innocent enough to simply have that meal, drink that beverage, buy those items, or enjoy that stranger, the cost is something you haven't considered yet. Your willpower was not strong enough to remain resolute, and now, you are paying the price: sacrificing your goals, ideals, or values.

Delayed Gratification

The opposite end of the spectrum is delayed gratification. This is when you consciously decide to work towards a larger goal with longer lasting benefits.

You delay the pleasures of now in favor of much larger enjoyment later. Like the marshmallow experiment or the chocolate cookies study, you use reason to conclude that if you can wait, you will receive an even greater reward.

Sounds easy? It isn't, not always.

For starters, delayed gratification can be much longer in time requirements than simply waiting 15 minutes to get two marshmallows. In the real world, we have to face societal obstacles, financial trials, and emotional battles to get to a reward that may only be reached a week, two months, or even years down the line. To weather the temptations that storm across your path while you move towards your goal requires a well-developed willpower.

It doesn't need an iron willpower. You may be heading towards your ultimate goal in a few years' time, but for now, you may also enjoy beneficial rewards along the way. This is why most diets even have a cheat day. It is a momentary pause to being so strict that allows you to relax and have a little harmless fun. As mentioned in Chapter 2, you do not have an infinite supply of willpower. So, you need to ration yourself, saving your willpower "credits" to use when it really matters. Having a well-trained willpower means you know when to use it or not. You evaluate each situation on a case-by-case merit system, deciding whether it is harmful or a harmless momentary distraction. Then, you make a judgment call.

Should you be consistent in your resolve and use your willpower well, you will be able to reach your goals while still having some fun along the way. Fun isn't the problem. Delayed gratification is about more than just fun though. It meets your inner need, instead of only satisfying your momentary wants.

Aristotle and most of the stoics wrote quite extensively about delayed gratification. It was then and is still a much-debated concept. What determines whether gratification is instant or delayed, and why should you favor delayed gratification? Much of the choice is ascribed to how developed your logic and willpower is. However, we must not lose sight of other factors such as your upbringing, social, and economic factors.

People who are poor tend to live hand to mouth. Perhaps since they lack future certainty, they choose to indulge in cheap thrills instead of saving for long-term advancement. This might explain why alcoholism and drug addiction is so prevalent among the poor classes or socio-economically challenged population groups. There is less of a chance of reaching some almost mythical future goal, so they grab at the first relief or thrill they can find. It may seem illogical to those who are not from that type of upbringing, but to those caught in the cycle of poverty—it makes perfect sense.

One other aspect to consider in the success of delayed gratification is the size of the reward in relation to the length of delay required. Getting $100 now is more desirable than getting $1,000 in five years' time. The reward does not outweigh the instant gratification. In this case, most people would choose the instant reward. After all, they might not even get anything in five years.

Delayed gratification is about doing the work needed now so you can get a reward in the future. It requires consistent and hard work. Instant gratification is about the now and feeling good right now. However, the tendency to slip into instant behavior is a threat to finding your North as it drags you further and further off course. Chasing instant thrills will become a habit that can have a very damning effect on your willpower.

Within the spectrum of gratification, we find different categories of temptation and reward we may face:

- **Food**

This is perhaps one of the most elementary of rewards. We use it on our children without even thinking. If you pass a difficult test, your mom might buy you a chocolate. When you pass your learners' exam, your mom might bake you a cake to celebrate. Even our bosses still use food as a reward token. When you get promoted at work, your boss may take you and your coworkers out to dinner.

Food was a reward for the primitive man. We can easily imagine the caveman bringing home a slaughtered buck to reward his tribe for their loyalty. Even birds make use of food as a reward and bribe. Male birds will offer food to a prospective mate. In this case, food has become an example of instant gratification. Whichever way you look at it, food is a powerful reward currency.

For those struggling with health issues, food can be both their heaven and hell. Most of us can quite easily resist eating a few chocolates now to lose some pounds for the holidays; however, when you have to resist eating certain foods for a prolonged period of time (perhaps even for the rest of your life), the temptation seems to increase. This is often why people struggle to overcome obesity. The delay and the nature of the reward seems too small for someone who needs to lose 100 pounds and keep that weight off for the rest of their lives. In this case, food is not a strong motivator for delayed gratification but rather a strong temptation instead.

- **Physical Pleasure**

We have become a world of people who want to feel good. As a result, smoking, drinking, casual sex, and chemical addictions are increasing at a shocking rate. Quitting is hard. You are probably surrounded by people who are still engaging in the activity you are trying to avoid. If you were a smoker, it is harder to quit when your friends are still smokers. Only when you are consistently assured your abstinence will yield future rewards, are you likely to resist temptation and quick thrills.

- **Satisfying Social Interactions**

The part of our brain that develops first is the primitive side. This is mostly our emotional centers, while our logical facilities such as the PFC only develop and mature much later. Hence, it is not difficult to see why teens tend to favor thrills that meet their emotional and social needs. Being part of the in-crowd may be way more meaningful to a teen than achieving the top academic position in their grade, for instance. This is then a classic case of instant gratification (short-term reward) opposed to delayed gratification (long-term reward).

- ## Money

Money makes the world go round—or so they say. We have it, and we spend it; however, we struggle to save it. This is because saving is a form of advanced delayed gratification. Most people only invest a fraction of their income in retirement plans, choosing to live now instead of setting aside for 40 years from now. Social media certainly doesn't help either. Open your mobile phone or social platforms like Facebook, Twitter, Instagram, and you are confronted by ways that entice you to spend money instead of saving it.

Securing your financial future for four decades from now when you are in your twenties may seem like a chase after the wind. You are unsure of whether you will even live long enough to enjoy the benefits of your retirement plans, and so, you spend and live in the now, forgetting the future. This is perhaps one of the hardest forms of delayed gratification.

- ## Achievement

In the end, our real goals reside in the future. They are all delayed. What we enjoy right now are temporary habits. When you are someone driven by achievement, you know the importance of delayed gratification. You will place a higher value on the future goal over the more immediate pleasure your habits could drive you to. So, making sure to create and follow good habits will help you tremendously in achieving your long-term goals.

Habits such as getting up early to walk or meditate will bring a greater calm and peace into your mind, enabling you to remain resolute in your convictions not to engage in temporary pleasures that may interfere with your long-term goals. Reading motivational books, engaging in self-esteem building tasks, and practicing to refuse what you don't normally value will help you maintain your willpower.

While forming healthy habits will enable you to make delayed gratification part of your modus operandi, it is also quite revealing to consider the reasons why people struggle so much to say no. I would suggest these considerations:

→ **Trying to Avoid Delay**

While you sit there, try to hold your breath. Do you notice how you become more anxious and uncomfortable the longer you hold your breath? Even though you know you can take another breath soon, you still feel upset at the delay in breath. This is the very reason why people engage in what is around them here and now. They prefer to allow themselves stuff as self-denial is uncomfortable. Instinct tells them to grab at what they can have right now. An example of this would be a beggar who spends their day's earnings to buy smokes and beer instead of putting it aside to buy something more meaningful.

→ **Uncertainty**

When you are a child, you are very trusting. You smile at strangers, hold hands with unknown individuals, and you even let people pick you up and swing you wildly without a care in the world. This is because you have complete trust in the world around you. However, as you age, and through a gazillion small but telling experiences, you begin to lose that trust. You realize the world isn't completely honest, and you lose faith in the world around you. As a result, you are filled with uncertainty. Not believing there will be opportunities or enough of what you need, you grasp at whatever is in reach, whether it is a bottle of booze, pills, or sex. Willpower requires self-control, and when you have this, you don't see yourself as a victim in the world, you can trust—you can trust yourself.

People who have come out of abusive relationships often struggle with feelings of uncertainty and insecurity. This affects how they make decisions, and what they view as being the way to negotiate for what they want in life.

→ **Age**

As previously mentioned, your age may reveal the level of mental maturity your brain has reached. Teens struggle to tame their emotions, while adults from 25 and up should start to be more in control of their willpower as their PFC develops. With age comes experience, and the more you experience, the more you learn. We can expect teens to engage in instant gratification as the driving force behind their decision-making paradigm. However, with adults, we tend to expect better and more long-term vision behind their actions as they have experienced more and should have learned from their mistakes.

→ **Imagination**

So, you want to show self-restraint to overcome the temptations of now and reach the ultimate goal in a much longer period's time? Using your imagination to help you sweeten the deal is a wonderful strategy for keeping your feet on the right path. Instead of drooling over that fresh donut at the coffee shop, you can rather redirect your imagination to see the beautiful dress you will be wearing to your friend's wedding in six months' time. If you can "see" your delayed reward, you will be less focused on the distractions of quick pleasures on offer.

➔ Higher Thinking

Having the mental smarts to envision your future means you will be able to reason out your way to get there. When you have a higher thinking ability, you can motivate yourself, and you can use strategies for keeping yourself on track to reach the finish line. However, if you are limited in your mental capacity or lack the smarts to really see your winding road to your goal future, then you will struggle to maintain a strong willpower. Plainly put, you will be overwhelmed by the temptation right at your feet.

While schooling is not necessarily an indication of smart thinking, it is often associated with higher cognitive thinking. People who have finished basic schooling tend to be more aware of long-term goals in their future planning, while high school dropouts tend to live in the immediate future, never planning for the goals that should sustain them through life like investing in an income protector or retirement annuity.

➔ Financial Status

When you have low financial means, you are less likely to reach your future goals. Simply put, your poverty limits your ability to focus on higher goals as you are trying to meet the most basic ones such as food, shelter, and acceptance for now. Maslow's famous hierarchy of needs clearly explains these needs as being pivotal to any future development. (However, Maslow also makes an allowance for the exception to any rule. There are certainly cases where people have risen from abject poverty to start thriving businesses or reached their higher goals in spite of their challenges.)

→ **Impulse Control**

Some of us have a shortened reaction time. Before we can even think, we have already begun doing something. The icing is already coating your lips before you even realize you have bitten into that slice of cake despite being on a diet. People with a low level of impulse control struggle to stay to the straight and narrow. Creating healthy habits are essential to helping them reach and maintain a steady willpower and goal driven path.

If your brakes aren't working, then you make sure not to drive too fast, and you may even have your hand on the emergency brake. Likewise, if you are someone who does before they think, then you would benefit from having a close friend help you avoid situations that you are vulnerable to, like sticking to you when a hot girl tempts you at the club and making sure you do not leave with her when you are already in a stable relationship.

→ **Emotional Awareness**

My friend had a new baby, and I was fascinated by how easy it was to calm the crying infant down. Simply stick a flavored pacifier into her mouth, and you're a-okay. Us adults are a bit like that too. When you are crying or feeling upset, you easily become pacified by a quick thrill on hand. Instant gratification seems to be exactly what you need as you feel emotionally overwhelmed and upset. However, once that quick reward has been used up, you are right back to feeling upset. My friend's baby soon began crying within a few minutes of having the pacifier in her mouth. Instant gratification wears off; its reward is not long lasting.

Instead of trying to self-soothe with instant rewards, rather focus on getting to the bottom of your feelings. Emotional awareness will help you assess where you are in your life, what you really need, and plan how you are going to achieve that need. This leads to delayed gratification—the long-term reward.

→   **Prevailing Moods**

The mood you are currently experiencing may provoke you into making a rash decision or giving in to temptation all the easier. When you are angry, depressed, or sad, you are more likely to yield to the lure of things you shouldn't do.

→   **The**   **Power**   **of Anticipation**

When we anticipate things, whether good or bad, we increase our tension levels. If you are holding out for something in the future that you feel negative about, you may find a way to negate that event. Like most of us decline going to the dentist, we end up pushing it aside for years instead of the six-monthly check-up.

With negative things, we postpone them, but with positive things we end up trying to rush into them or find ways to accelerate our reward date, even if that means cutting corners we shouldn't.

So, while you may use anticipation as a good force, utilizing your imagination to build the image of your future goal, it is not always a good thing when you are feeling stressed or lonely or depressed. Your anticipation may simply overwhelm your resolve instead of boosting it.

The Benefits of Delayed Gratification

Being able to delay your need for gratification has been linked to the personality traits of successful people. You will be more likely to achieve your long-term goals as you focus on the end result and not momentary relief along the way. This doesn't mean you don't ever enjoy immediate gratification. Instead, it simply means you choose wisely, making smaller temptations part of your progress and not the reason for your failure.

You begin to focus on longer-term goals instead of transient pleasures. While having a glass of wine with friends after work is enjoyable, you choose to do so sparingly, rather choosing to focus on getting your work done or preparing for your future goals.

By keeping that "hunger" in you to reach for the goals you set in your future, you build the energy to forge forward. The occasional temptation may be chosen to help maintain some balance. However, you don't let the immediate thrill or momentary easing of your pains break your momentum.

Knowing you are strong enough to withstand senseless temptations will fill you with a sense of achievement. Being able to reach your goals and enjoy that delayed gratification will also deepen your feeling of accomplishment. When you feel good, your body responds in kind. People who are better at engaging in delayed gratification tend to enjoy better health, experiencing fewer cases of diabetes, heart complications, or eating disorders. In essence, when you can hold out for what matters, you begin to experience benefits to your health and a sense of purpose and accomplishment.

Lastly, I want you to imagine someone who is known for being on the fence about everything in their life. We've all met someone like this—a person who can't make up their mind about anything and scurries off into a hundred directions while never getting anywhere. Perhaps you know someone like this, and perhaps you are someone like this. Being with someone who is indecisive, lacks conviction, and doesn't know what they want is terrible for the people around them. We naturally gravitate towards strong leader personalities— the people who know what they want. As a result, people who are able to control themselves and use the necessary restraint to avoid harmful instant gratification (while holding out for delayed gratification) are popular among other people. Since you are constantly self-communicating, you also become really good at being empathetic and aware of life challenges. These are endearing qualities and perhaps the best benefit of delayed gratification as a lifestyle.

Why It's So Hard to Wait

Quite simply put, we lack patience. If we look at the Oxford Marketing Dictionary's definition of delayed gratification, we will find that delayed gratification isn't just about waiting but more about waiting *patiently* for the reward or gratification. We lack patience. We live in a society where we are conditioned to want everything now. If you want to have your money transferred now—simply pay an extra fee and boom! Want your takeaway food now? Just go to the drive through. You don't even have to get out of your car; it's already there for you as soon as you've paid. We lack the ability to wait. This leads to a lack of self-restraint.

Our society encourages instant gratification. Everything is geared to being faster, giving pleasure quicker, and having what we want as soon as possible. Patience is a virtue, but it's one we no longer cultivate. Like little kids who keep asking "Are we there yet?" We don't enjoy the journey, only wanting to be at our goal or destination immediately. Sadly, this has several negative impacts on our lives and our belief systems.

Life becomes faster and faster, and as a result, we lose many important values along the way. Since we have unlearned the ability to wait, we have learned to place little value on anything long term; instead, chasing after the quick rewards offered by instant gratifications. In our consumerist society, this is becoming the norm. We struggle to hold out for a more permanent future reward, especially since that reward may never materialize anyway.

If we look at the education sector, we can see this problem hard at work. Most universities and colleges experience massive dropout rates. While some students may drop out due to financial difficulties, most simply give up. They struggle to hold themselves to a difficult course with the promised reward at the end of a long and arduous journey. Since they doubt they will be able to finish their chosen course, they often give up within the first or second year of studies, not wanting to "waste" more time on such an unsure endgame reward. The uncertainty makes people choose to give up on delayed gratification, choosing instant gratification instead. After all, instant gratification is here and now, and you can enjoy the rewards immediately (like quitting school and finding a day job where you get money at the end of the month), while you could have failed school and lost out on those instant rewards anyway. Staying the course takes patience, courage, and dedication. It takes willpower.

Willpower isn't something you are simply born with, nor is it something you magically develop when you need it. It is like any muscle in your body, and if you develop it from childhood, you will have all the skills you need later in life to be patient and work towards a delayed goal with self-control. Your whole life is made up of tasks to help you develop this skill. Even waiting for your gifts as a child (when those gifts have been under the Christmas tree for weeks) is an example of patience and delayed gratification.

As an adult, it is possible to rebuild the atrophied willpower muscles by guiding yourself through a similar process of wait and reward, work and enjoy, patience and delayed gratification. This process requires that you follow a specific series of strategies to help you with this mental workout.

Strategies to Increase Your Ability to Delay Gratification

As with most things in life, having a strategy will help you get there. Plunging ahead without planning or deciding about your goals is not likely to serve you well. Here are some efficient strategies I have tested in my own journey through delayed gratification and willpower:

- **Worthy Goals**

Pursue goals that are worth your time, effort, and patience. If they are meaningful enough, you will be more inclined to invest into them, develop the patience to obtain them, and diligently work towards them. Some worthy goals include working towards a stable and loving relationship, working to achieve your business goals, studying for that degree you need for the job you've always wanted, and saving for that holiday you've been dreaming of.

- **Set the Finish Line Date**

When the finish line is unclear or so distant you can't see it, you will be less likely to persevere. If you are studying, you can even break that end goal down into the number of years your studies will take. Setting such a vague future goal as wanting a six-figure salary per month when you are only in high school at the moment is an example of a goal you will struggle to visualize.

When you visualize your goal, you need to be able to see every detail of it, every step of the road, and every commitment you will make along the way. It can't just be about you seeing yourself driving a fancy car, dating supermodels, and having a big salary. Those are all transient pleasures, and you haven't created a step-by-step plan for reaching that future yet. So be specific, set dates, mile markers, and all the steps you will take. This will help you track your progress. Celebrate with smaller gratifications to help sustain your willpower and formulate contingency plans when the unexpected happens.

- ## **Say No to Band-Aids**

Getting ahead in life is not a quick fix process. While you may be working towards a goal that is tougher than anything you've ever faced in your life, you could be tempted to seek temporary relief from the pain, fatigue, or discomfort you are being forced to endure. Don't. Simply don't.

Having a night out with a stranger will not help you fix or build a long-term relationship (if that was your goal). While it may temporarily make you forget about the arguments you've had, it will not bring your partner closer to you. Taking time off to go away on holiday when your business is floundering will not help you get back on track. And while you may feel better for a moment, you will end up returning to a business that is still in trouble (and the additional cost of that impulsive holiday spend). You'd be better served by investing in the profound change that will help you get to the bottom of the problems you are trying to fix.

- ## **Make Gratitude Part of Your Day**

It is so easy to lose focus. When you are looking at a journey of a thousand miles, it becomes harder to see the end. By seeing where you are and practicing active mindfulness, you will engage in real gratitude. Gratitude can also become a means for tracking your progress, for building positive energy, and for maintaining your forward momentum to reach your goal or delayed gratification. During your day, if you force yourself to find something to be genuinely grateful for, you will begin to see the struggle isn't all bad or endless.

• The Seinfeld Strategy

Allegedly explained by comedian Jerry Seinfeld (who produces a prolific amount of comedy work each year), it boils down to working consistently, not giving yourself the option to simply evaluate and give up. The strategy suggests you take a wall calendar and mark each day with a cross if you have worked on that day. The goal is to build an uninterrupted chain of crosses (James Clear, n.d.). It isn't about doing good work or excellent work; instead, it is just about working. The goal is to be productive, never giving yourself the excuse to slack off as this breaks the chain of crosses. Consistently working brings you one step closer to achieving the delayed gratification of your goal. I remember driving behind a car with a bumper sticker that summed this up quite brilliantly: God, I'll put in the quantity, if You'll take care of the quality.

In your quest to increase your ability to be patient and delay gratification, you will need some emergency strategies too. These are there to help you when you feel like you're about to fall off the wagon. For recovering alcoholics, this strategy might look something like calling your sponsor when you are standing outside a bar and feeling tempted. These strategies will help you cross off each day in a positive way and not break the consistency of the cross-chains that Seinfeld explained.

• Empathize and Apologize to Your Future Self

When you are tempted to go for that instant gratification, you can begin to see your future self being disappointed that you caved in. Imagine your future self looking at your current self with disappointment in your eyes. No one likes a lame excuse, and your future self will not be impressed to hear you dropped out from college because you preferred to party with friends. If you have enough imagination, you can even see your future self-suffering as a result of your instant gratification slips. Suddenly, that night out when you should be studying becomes less tempting.

You can even try this exercise if you are repeatedly tempted by instant pleasures. Write a letter of apology to your future self. Try to list the reasons why you engaged in temptations continuously. Also write down all the ways you have disappointed your future self. Explain how you are going to make it right to your future self. Sometimes, having a promise on paper helps us to focus better and stay on track. You could even carry the letter with you, and each time you are tempted by an instant gratification, you can take the letter out and reread it. In essence, it makes you stop and think. Temptation feeds on our emotional needs, but it quickly vanishes when we apply the ointment of logical thinking to it.

If you know you are going to be surrounded by temptations that could cause you to stray, then you might be well-served by setting up some personal laws beforehand. These are convictions that you have prepared in advance of temptation. It makes it easier for your willpower to not be strained when you have certain things you don't see as negotiable. If you have it as a non-negotiable that you won't be drinking and driving or that you will never double cross a business partner, then you will be less likely to be tempted by these.

It is almost like pattern recognition to your brain. You associate the temptation with the preplanned response, taking the thinking out of it.

- **Subdivide and Conquer**

Imagine going to college or university for a four-year degree, but instead of receiving your results every semester and graduating from each year till you have obtained your degree, you only get rewards or progress reports when the four years are up. Such a system is unfathomable. You would be completely lost without milestones or other levels of accomplishment to bolster your confidence and help you track your progress towards meeting your ultimate goal and the delayed gratification that comes with it.

In real life, we need smaller markers to help us remain on track. So, when a goal seems too distant, you would benefit from creating smaller or shorter subgoals. Like breadcrumbs on the road through the forest, these will help you stay on track, achieve the subgoals, and finally, reach the main goal. After all, we all need feedback to track our progress, make changes if necessary, and get those little confidence boosts along the way.

- **Evaluate Your Emotions**

Temptation thrives when our emotions go on a rampage. When you feel yourself saying "I want to..." rather replace that statement with "I feel..." You will begin to see that temptations are really masks for our nastier emotions. Want to eat that cookie? You might be feeling lonely. Want to spend the money you have been saving for your business venture on a weekend in Vegas? You might be feeling tired and overwhelmed by your workload instead.

Knowing your emotions will help you defang your temptations. Make the conscious choice to know how you **feel** before you try to get what you **want**.

- **Self-Talk Matters**

Often, if we listen carefully, we will hear our inner voice urging us to either give in to temptation or resist it. Start listening to your self-talk. If you are negative and running yourself down, you will be more likely to engage in self-defeating behavior such as going for instant gratification. However, if you can listen to your inner voice, argue with it when it is negative, and change it to be a more positive and encouraging voice, you will find the focus being inward where you can plan and hope, instead of outward where temptation dwells.

- **Negotiate an If-Then Arrangement**

Ok, so completely avoiding temptations is virtually impossible. When you do slip up and engage in a cheap thrill, you end up feeling worthless and it may actually cause you to fall off the wagon completely. While you should still try to resist any temptations that may potentially cause you to fail, such as a recovering alcoholic not taking a drink, you could enter into negotiation mode. This allows you to minimize the damage done by a temptation slip.

Choosing to have a small temptation now can be offset by saying "if this ..., then I'll ...." So, if you are dieting and want a cookie, you can tell yourself, "If I eat this cookie, then I'll do twenty squats to work off the extra calories." If you are tempted by a weekend away with friends when you should be working at your new business venture, then you could reason as follows: "If I take the weekend off, then next weekend I will work extra hours to make up for the lag in workload."

You are asserting logic and removing emotion from your decisions. This means self-control remains present, and you are actually making choices instead of having a breakdown in control. Your willpower remains strong then.

While the ultimate goal is to build up a stern resolve that is still flexible enough to let life be fun, you should use this to create powerful and sustaining habits. Though you can negotiate, set goals, break goals down into smaller markers, and avoid temptations, you do want to be able to choose sometimes and rely on habits at other times. Surely, you do not want to think about every tempting treat you see all day? Having positive and powerful habits in place to control your behavior will help take a load off your self-control and leave your willpower free to focus on more important threats to your long-term gratification goals.

Chapter 6:

Willpower Is Just the Beginning— Building Good Habits

I have a friend who is more than a little clumsy, and I had to take him to the doctor to have a broken finger set. Now, if you have ever broken a finger before, then you'd know it's a particularly stubborn body part to break. For starters, once broken, it needs to heal, but to heal, it needs to stay straight. Problem is, fingers want to bend. It's what they are made to do, and bending is ingrained into them. After all, they have been doing it for most of your life. So, how do you get that finger to stay straight? How do you undo habits you've spent a lifetime creating?

Looking at the doctor carefully placing the finger guard around the broken finger before applying layers and layers of casting bandages, I had an epiphany. You see, the broken finger was rather dumb. If left to its own devices, it would probably grow on skew. So, medical science had realized early on that to help that stubborn finger find the right thing to do and stick to doing it, you needed to tape the broken finger to a strong finger.

It's the same with us and our damaging habits. When we want to create a new habit, or heal from a habit that breaks us, we need support too. New habits need to be repeated, and the best way to make sure you don't break these fragile first growths is to tape the new habit to an existing habit or strength.

While you begin with willpower and self-control, you need to make these into habits or you will simply end up with skew ideas and broken efforts. It is not an easy process, and like the broken finger of my clumsy friend, you will also have to put some repeated effort into growing in line with the form of the cast you will be creating. It will take time. A finger takes around six weeks to heal from a fracture. Developing a new habit commonly follows the 21/90 timeframe. This means it takes 21 days to form the habit, but 90 days for that habit to become automatic.

Back to the finger: if you remove your cast too soon, you will end up with a finger bending right back into the crooked shape, or worse, with a fracture that never attaches itself properly. The same holds true for your habits. If you remove the controlling and guiding principles too soon, you will revert right back to negative behaviors and temptation yielding. So, how do you build habits that will help you assist your willpower?

Understanding Willpower

Forming a new habit takes a substantial amount of willpower initially. When you don't quite know how your willpower works, it will be harder to succeed. Understanding that willpower is finite and that you create and reinforce your willpower by developing self-control and healthy habits will help you form lasting habits. Simply willing something to be is not enough. It is a conscious decision to do something that may not be easy at first, and it may certainly become a challenge two weeks into the 21/90-day timeframe.

If you wanted to cultivate the habit of eating pancakes for breakfast every day, you would probably be quite enthusiastic right through. There hardly seems to be a downside to it, right? Wrong? For starters, eating the same food every day for 21 days will become boring. If it's that hard with something you like, imagine doing it with something that is hard like going for a five-mile run before work every day or cutting out bread from your diet. This means you require a conscious effort to maintain difficult habits.

You also need strategies in place when you start to lose the motivation to persevere with the activity you want to make into a habit. When you are being tempted to give up, you need to have an arsenal of ideas and methods to help you pull yourself up out of the ditch of instant gratifications. You can form healthy habits—here's how:

Habit Formation

Forming habits takes time. You don't wake up in the morning and suddenly you are ready and able to perform an activity you have never done before. Instead, it takes time to mold your behavior into a new and productive habit. The biggest poison to habit formation is when you give up or you quit because you wanted rewards much sooner than is really possible. Using the Seinfeld strategy might be useful here to track your progress. Using your wall calendar, you can indicate when you start the new habit, marking off each day where you didn't relent in your habit formation. Each time you slip up and act against your new habit, you should restart the calendar.

This calendar should also become a physical representation of your mental state. Habits start in your mind before they are acted on. If you want to lose weight, it isn't about the diet. You first need to get your brain right, get your mind fully committed to the goal before you start cutting carbs or counting calories.

Without your mind's commitment, you will fall short on consistency. It is not about doing big things every so often. Rather, forming a positive habit to help support your willpower and achieve your dreams is about showing up every day and working at it every day. The key is consistency!

Turning Willpower Into Long-Term Habits

Converting some of your willpower or that continuous decision-making capacity of your mind into habit is about taking some of the work out of life for you. The idea is to have your willpower available to deal with other matters as they arise. This can help cut down on temptation, decrease stress, and limit wasting of your willpower. By investing some willpower daily for a predefined period of time (the 21/90-day rule), you will be able to have a skilled habit that returns that energy daily.

Making habits is a process. You do not simply wake up in the morning and decide you will be saying no to all the wasteful expenses you no longer like. Picking a habit to form can't be done willy-nilly. It isn't done to keep up with the Joneses, and it isn't done to meet some public opinion of you. Instead, you should identify an aspect of your life where you would benefit from some healthy autopilot help. After all, you want to free up your willpower eventually after training up this new assistant (habit) you will use.

So, you should pick habits you will benefit from. If your health is failing or not as good as it should be, you could start with a plan to reach your new health goals. Jumping in feet first will not necessarily help you succeed. If you need to lose 40 pounds and get fit, you will fail if you start running around the block every day. No? How often have you seen people start a habit only to fall flat?

There are several strategies to habit formation you could use to help you. Each of these will help you embrace and internalize your habit, making it a part of your thinking, feeling, and being. I found in my life I needed to sometimes write down my habits and where I was going wrong or doing well, recapping, reflecting, and retrying different approaches. Put in the effort, but do not be like a mindless mule who slugs ahead and never thinks about where it is going. You have a destination, a goal, and you should approach this process with eyes and mind open to learn, change, and grow.

Think About It

Take some time to reflect on the habit you want to build. Ask yourself tough questions before you invest time into something you have chosen for the wrong reasons. First, check your HALT status to make sure you are in the right state of mind to make decisions and choose actions now. Assess whether your hunger is being met, whether your anger isn't playing a factor in your decision, and whether your loneliness isn't instigating a new habit that you will not be able to fulfill. Lastly, never make important decisions when you are tired (whether physical or emotional).

Here are some questions I also asked myself when I was finding my way to building the ultimate willpower and forming habitual skills in my life:

1. Why did I choose this habit?

2. How will this habit help my life?

3. Is this the most simplistic form of the skill or habit?

4. Which other habits like this have I already mastered?

5. Should I choose this habit? Is it worth the effort?

6. How will I add this habit to my life and make it my own?

Thought is powerful, and you should spend enough time planning, considering, and strategizing. Once you know you have chosen the right habit, you can begin to consider what steps to take, plan where you will check your progress, and how you will succeed at making it YOUR habit. Each of us create habits in our own way.

I often think of that iconic moment in the 1993 movie *Cool Runnings* when Sanca realizes that he (and his bobsledding team) can't adopt habits that belong to another team; they need to form their own motto and habit. You also need to find your own way to choose, grow, and embrace your habits. This all starts in your head.

Engage in regular self-monitoring. Check if your new habit is growing steadily and identify any factors hampering your progress. Plan what you will be doing to help your habit thrive. Like a new seedling with its own need to grow, your habit requires things like praise, energy, interest, and novelty to flourish.

Does It Matter?

Once you have decided on a habit to cultivate, you can begin to integrate that habit into your life. With every action you take, you can ask yourself whether that action matters. If your chosen habit is to only choose food and drinks that benefit your health, then you can ask yourself if packing a healthy lunch matters. Yes, it does, so you do it. You ask yourself if having drinks after work will help your body stay healthy. No, it doesn't, so you don't do it.

This line of questioning can also be applied to other habits in your life, helping you return to the core values of those habits. If you have decided to habitually show integrity in your work life, then you can ask yourself if cheating a colleague out of their promotion helps you meet your habit of honesty. No, it doesn't, so you don't do it.

Only when you know the nature of the chosen habit will you be able to ask yourself if it matters. This allows you to know whether it is worth investing further into a habit or not. Once your mind makes peace with these questions, it becomes your second nature, and it reduces the mental noise that normally confuses and corrupts our choices.

Further, be sure to choose a habit that is dependent on you, not on others. You can only take actions that are within your power to take. If the habit you want to create is to have friends, you are heading towards failure. You can't decide for other people, and you can't force them to be your friends. This is wishful thinking, not habit formation. Instead, you can choose to be a good friend to the people in your life, to be friendly and considerate to others. These things are within your power, and you can be responsible for them. Making money can't be a habit as this is a circumstance or outside event beyond your reach. You can choose to work every day and earn a living as a habit. Only choose actions that are within your power to act on. Habits are about you, not about the people around you.

Shift Your Focus

Forming a habit requires quite a bit of effort and energy, so you should choose a habit that offers you long-term benefits. If your habit is to lose weight, you will probably come up short as it is a habit that has a short lifespan. After all, you can't continue to lose weight until you are dead. Instead, look further ahead, choosing a habit that offers future potential from day one. Forming the habit of eating healthily will help you lose weight, but you can continue this habit until you are 100 years old.

Avoid choosing a habit that is about a quick fix. Trying to lose weight by following a crash diet will perhaps succeed for a short while, but that habit will not have any real future value as it can't be sustained continuously or long term. Rather focus on a habit that has lasting benefits.

Many supposed strategies and concepts on offer in our commercial world often claim to have wonder cures or products, and you need to be aware that manipulations have a habit of backfiring on consumers. Positive change will help you succeed.

Shift your focus from the now and focus on what you want in the future. Find a way to link your present experience with your desired future self. This is the habit you need to form. If you start to lose the habit, you can imagine yourself practicing this habit now and in the future, affirming its value to you.

Small Steps

We love dramatic examples, and this may cause us to seek drastic steps to take when really, we need to use a slow but steady approach. Your chosen habit may be to work productively every day since you want to one day have your own business. You will not be able to maintain 16-hour work days, so don't try to do that. Instead, you can create the healthy smaller steps such as working an extra hour at the end of your regular work day to build your business dream. Every effort, no matter how small, contributes to your goal. Your habit is not to have a business (that's a goal); instead, your habit is to work productively every day. That productive work can take any form as long as you habitually do it every day.

Overfacing yourself will not help you sustain the habit of productivity though. Instead, you will make much more headway when you break your habit down into smaller steps. I saw this in action recently in a video that went viral online of a tortoise playing ball with a dog. I had always considered a tortoise to be a slow animal that never seemed to get anywhere, but when I saw how those little steps could really cause this animal to motor after what it wanted, I was amazed. Keeping those little beady eyes on the prize, the tortoise followed a process of step, step, and repeat. It moved much faster than I had imagined with those little steps, and you can also make progress with small steps at a time.

While one action may stick out in memory, having a pattern of actions will linger longer, becoming a habit. So, aim not for one single action or step but rather for a repetition of steps for a lengthy time. Like the tortoise in the video, you can also claim your goal by stepping continuously.

Stack Good Habits

Remember the broken finger I told you about? To get the bone to knit straight, the doctor had taped it to the healthy fingers next to it. This is exactly what you should do with your habits. Take a habit that already works for you and hitch the new habit to it. In practice, this will help you commit and form new patterns of habitual behavior. If you have the habit of drinking a cup of coffee or tea before work, then you can link this to the habit of mindful minutes in the morning too. As you sip your warm beverage, you can intentionally clear your mind of worries and doubts that cloud your day.

Other examples of habit stacking may include:

→ Combining your morning dressing routine with dictating your daily to-do list so you have more time at the office.

→ Following your morning breakfast with a walk around your house to get your daily steps up.

→ Inviting a possible business contact to your regular after-work drinks once a week.

→ While you pour your bath at night, you can use the time it takes for the tub to do some stretching exercises to improve your mobility.

➜ Stack the habit of your morning commute to work with loud singing in the car to release some stress before you enter the busy workday.

The key here is to use a habit that already exists daily in your life and tie it to the new habit you want to create. If the first habit is already consistent, then the new habit will follow the same pattern. Habits need repetition to become formed. You already have the repetitions in place with the first habit, so simply add the new habit, guiding it into place like the broken finger with its buddy fingers holding it up.

Novelty Tasks

If we consider learning strategies, we will find that psychologists have consistently recommended that learning needs to remain novel for it to capture your brain's interest. If you do something over and over, you will become pretty bored with it should that task be boring already. Learning will not happen.

Novelty or excitement is a powerful learning aid. By choosing tasks or habits that are novel to acquire, you will increase your chances of the habit sticking. Take exercising daily as a habit. If you do the same exercise routine every day, you will soon be bored to tears. This is why most fitness trainers have special days for specific muscle groups. The novelty creates interest and you more readily commit to the new task. Variety also helps on this front. If you want to go walking around your neighborhood every day, then choosing a different route for each day of the week will help you do it more easily. Walking the same route daily will soon become uninteresting, and your brain will protest by "forgetting" to go for your walk.

If you are creative and preplan your habit per week, you will be able to ensure you maintain the novel element, keeping your mind interested and improving your self-control and commitment to the new habit.

When you are busy engineering your life, you need to maintain interest in your actions. Your brain will begin to see your involvement in its habits as boring if you are boring. So, rather choose to do novel things every day. Keep your brain interested in these habits by doing something new and exciting.

Reward Yourself

We all love to be rewarded for our hard-won efforts. If you want a reward, you will likely have to look inward for praise. This is your habit, after all, and you aren't going to find anyone out there who will reward you for your progress. Instead, the habit is yours to own and celebrate. You need to meet the desire for reward that is so natural to us all. Good work should receive rewards, so when you work at your habit formation, you should also include token rewards or mile markers to celebrate.

Positive reinforcement (reward) works. Motivation (or the energy and interest to keep up with a habit) is increased by reward. However, some habits may take a long time to bear any fruits. If you are habitually working late to get a promotion, you may have to do so for a year or more. Should you be eating healthily to lose weight, you may need several months of this to start seeing weight loss. In the meantime, you may begin to lose hope, believing your efforts to be in vain. This is where your own reward structure will help you stay focused and goal driven.

You can include smaller goals within your habit formation, celebrating its success with a reward. Your late nights of work can be rewarded by taking a small holiday after three weeks. Remember that it takes 90 days to form and operationalize (or habitualize) a new habit. Your rewards should be spread throughout that timeframe. Setting reward goals that exceed your current motivation levels will become pointless.

Working longer hours to build up a new business? Your rewards could be to take an off-day every week, followed by a weekend away once a month. Trying to follow a healthy lifestyle? Your rewards could include a cheat day once a week. This could be extended into a monthly party where you invite your friends to share some decadent foods with you. Choose a reward that excites you during your planning phase. The more accessible the reward, the more motivated you will be by the consistent reception of it. This also helps teach you the value of delayed gratification and builds your self-control and willpower as a result.

Account for Yourself

Rewards are wonderful, but if you are to complete the spectrum of psychological reinforcement, you need to consider negative reinforcement and even punishment. You are training your mind into accepting a new habit, and like a parent raising their child, you need to instill positive learning with positive rewards, discourage negative actions with negative reinforcement. Punishment is not likely to succeed as it has a severely negative connotation to it.

If you have set a habit such as working longer hours daily to build your business, yet you have gone home feeling sick or tired for the last three days, then you need to take appropriate action to correct the behavior that is not building this habit. Firstly, consider whether you are suffering from HALT, and take action to remedy this by eating more or better food, acknowledging your emotional state, socializing a little before putting in the extra time, and napping for a few minutes to rest before doing the work. However, if the HALT method has been met, you need to consider other possibilities. Negative reinforcement means you hold yourself accountable for your failure. Perhaps you add an additional half hour to the next few days of extra work to make up for lost time. Perhaps you remove one reward from your day if you fail to follow the habit you are building. Spend five minutes seeing your business in ruins in the future due to your lack of effort. See yourself apologizing to your family for letting them down. This negative reinforcement will spur you to renew your efforts.

Replace Motivation

While being motivated is essential to building healthy habits, maintaining that level of motivation may not be possible. HALT factors start to influence your motivation, and you may find yourself feeling deflated pretty soon. If you are working longer hours to create a part-time business in addition to your day job, you will have to fight off fatigue, emotional highs and lows, isolation, and even hunger. This could all lead to you becoming demotivated.

A strategy that yields great rewards is to replace your motivation. You could scatter your life with little reminders, rewards, tasks, and game plans to help you focus and commit to your goals. Placing sticky notes on your mirror at home or on your steering wheel will help you to just take a breath before changing gears as you pursue your goals. Prepare yourself that there will be days when your motivation wanes, and you need to accept those days as long as they don't become the norm. Find ways to boost your motivation levels by taking walks, reading good books, talking to positive people, or even eating a candy bar once in a while.

Remember that you are not alone in this life, and you can turn to others to help lift you up or cheer you up when your motivation reaches flat broke levels.

The Joy Yardstick

A life without joy is a life not worth living. Even though it is hard work to reach your goals, and it is incredibly draining to maintain your willpower and self-discipline, you should still enjoy your life. Sometimes, when depression or fatigue hits, you may start to wonder if it is all worth it in the end. Certainly, answering that question may produce a less than favorable answer when you are tired and overwhelmed.

Making gratitude a part of your life can help you maintain some perspective. When you make reflection a daily event, you allow yourself to find the joy of your day and celebrate this by increasing your motivation. If you can identify even one moment of contentment, happiness, or joy in your day, then you can focus on that feeling and sustain yourself when the going gets tough.

Initially, you may be quite overwhelmed when you are creating a new habit. It can be difficult to sustain, and while you have just learned some valuable skills and strategies here, you may still feel quite lost when you set out or when you hit that first bump in the road. The following questions and checklist are designed to help you get back on track, keep moving forward, and reach your habit goals.

Habit Q&A

1. Is this habit meaningful to your life?
2. How do you feel when you are practicing this habit?
3. Name three joy feelings you get when you practice this habit.
4. What is your motivation for this habit?
5. Where is your focus directed for this habit?

Habit Checklist

❑ Did you link this habit to an existing habit?
❑ Is it meaningful to you right now? Can you make it meaningful right now?
❑ Did you plan on paper?
❑ Are you focusing forward?
❑ Take smaller steps.

❑ Could you link this habit to a different existing habit to help support it?

❑ Did you make it novel and interesting?

❑ Have you chosen meaningful rewards scheduled at appropriate intervals?

❑ When you fail, did you question yourself? Did you make up for failure, thereby nullifying the lack of progress and moving forward?

❑ Which motivation substitutes and reinforcements did you use? Sticky notes, books, chats, bright flowers, good music, dancing around while you do taxes?

❑ Measure joy.

Conclusion

Everything in life requires willpower. It is a commitment to finish what we start. Even reading this book required some willpower. When things are easy or fun, like eating cake, we can easily finish what we start. However, when the going is a bit more challenging, we need to focus and show self-control and perseverance as we forge ahead.

Self-control and motivation are all parts that make up willpower, and as you have discovered, we can learn these. Like muscles on an athlete, we can train them, improve them, strengthen them, and refine them. If you were to enter into a race against Marion Jones, one of America's top sprint athletes of all time, you would probably lose without him even breaking a sweat. This is partly due to him having developed the muscles to run faster than you. He is merely using a fraction of his strength and agility. Running has become his habit, and he can do it without even thinking.

Likewise, in my life, I cultivated habits to serve my willpower needs. Today, I can achieve things that baffle my colleagues without seeming to break a sweat. This is because I have also created habits that can serve my willpower. I have shared the road to habit formation and improved willpower with you in this book.

You Are Skilled

Having read this book, you are now ready to put all these strategies and the knowledge herein into practice. And practice makes perfect. You will probably have a few false starts, and you will have down days when you simply feel like a giant flop. Don't lose heart; you can persevere. You can create the habits to support and enrich your willpower, and you can reach any goals you decide to set yourself with the methods in this book.

You have learned the theory behind the concept of a willpower, discovering where it forms in your brain, and you also learned that it isn't finite. I encourage you to strengthen your willpower, and you can do it! Using the HALT paradigm, you are now able to question yourself and see where and what is draining your willpower.

Goal setting, knowing your limits, and pushing them, as well as acknowledging and dealing with temptation is now familiar territory to you. While you are probably itching to launch forward into developing incredible willpower and accomplishing amazing things, I encourage you to maintain a balance and take care of your body and mind.

By embracing delayed gratification, you can train your willpower and begin to form healthy habits. Through knowledge and training, you will begin to struggle less with waiting and be more eager in reaching goals. With dedication and repetitions, you will begin to turn willpower into a healthy and lasting habit. Then, the world is your oyster!

Willpower Is Made to Share

You know what to do, now do it! Willpower doesn't work on its own; you need to get out there and work it. When your steps falter, use the checklists and go to the relevant sections of this book. You have all the knowledge of what to do and how to do it.

Willpower is made to share. When you find something good and true, you automatically have an urge to tell someone. I urge you to tell others about the skills, strategies, and knowledge of this book. Please share the gift of willpower on Amazon.com by leaving a kind review or sharing on social media.

References

Ackerman, C. E. (2020). *What is Instant Gratification? A Definition + 16 Examples and Quotes*. Positive Psychology. https://positivepsychology.com/instant-gratification/

Calarco, J. M. (2018). *Why Rich Kids Are So Good at the Marshmallow Test*. The Atlantic. https://www.theatlantic.com/family/archive/2018/06/marshmallow-test/561779/

Cherry, K. (2020). *Phineas Gage's Astonishing Brain Injury*. Very Well Mind. https://www.verywellmind.com/phineas-gage-2795244

Cummins, D. (2013). *How to Boost Your Willpower: Willpower Is Like a Muscle—in More Ways Than One*. Psychology Today. https://www.psychologytoday.com/za/blog/good-thinking/201306/how-boost-your-willpower

Eyal, N. (November 23, 2016). *Have We Been Thinking About Willpower the Wrong Way for 30 Years?* Harvard Business Review. https://hbr.org/2016/11/have-we-been-thinking-about-willpower-the-wrong-way-for-30-years

James Clear.com. (n.d.). *How to Stop Procrastinating on Your Goals by Using the "Seinfeld Strategy."* https://jamesclear.com/stop-procrastinating-seinfeld-strategy

Kabir, H. (n.d.). *Can Too Much Willpower Be Bad for You?* Happify Daily. https://www.happify.com/hd/can-too-much-willpower-be-bad-for-you/

Kokkoris, M. D., & Stovrova, O. (2020). *The Dark Side of Self-Control.* Harvard Business Review. https://hbr.org/2020/01/the-dark-side-of-self-control

Lino, C. (2020). *The Psychology of Willpower: Training the Brain for Better Decisions.* Positive Psychology. https://positivepsychology.com/psychology-of-willpower/

The British Psychological Society. (2015). *New Research Challenges the Idea That Willpower Is a "Limited Resource."* Research Digest. https://digest.bps.org.uk/2015/06/24/new-research-challenges-the-idea-that-willpower-is-a-limited-resource/

Tunikova, O. (2018). *The Science of Willpower: How to Train Your Productivity Muscle.* Medium. https://medium.com/@tunikova_k/the-science-of-willpower-how-to-train-your-productivity-muscle-8b2738ce745b

Valentine, M. (2018). *Learn the "HALT" Method to Control Your Impulses and Stay Focused Longer.* Goalcast. https://www.goalcast.com/2018/10/24/learn-halt-method-control-impulses/

Van Edwards, V. (n.d.). *Increase Your Willpower With These 10 Scientific Strategies.* Science of People. https://www.scienceofpeople.com/willpower/

Villarica, H. (2012). *Modern Conception of Willpower.* The Atlantic. https://www.theatlantic.com/health/archive/2012/04/the-chocolate-and-radish-experiment-that-birthed-the-modern-conception-of-willpower/255544/#:~:text=Back%20in%201996%2C%20Roy%20Baumeister,experiment%20that%20was%20downright%20evil.&text=In%20the%20first%20part%20of,alongside%20other%20chocolate-flavored%20confections.

Willard, C. (2017). *A Simple Strategy for Creating New Habits.* Mindful: Healthy Mind, Healthy Life. https://www.mindful.org/science-halting-old-habits/

www.ingramcontent.com/pod-product-compliance
Lightning Source LLC
Chambersburg PA
CBHW020258030426
42336CB00010B/826